COURTNEY SIMONE

The Entrepreneurial Guide to Success Part 1

For New & Aspiring Entrepreneurs

Contains explicit language suitable for ages 16+

First edition

ISBN: 978-1-7338530-9-5

This book was professionally typeset on Reedsy.
Find out more at reedsy.com

Contents

1

Introduction

For the past year, my DMs have been flooded with people asking for entrepreneurial advice and guidance. I am flattered to be a trusted source for many as they embark on their journey into entrepreneurship. It took a lot of sleepless nights, wasted time and money, getting scammed, discipline, and sacrifice to get where I am today. To guide the next boss babe or boss bro on how to create generational wealth is such an honor.

Allow me to introduce myself. I am THEE Courtney Simone. I emphasize my name with THEE, because although my name may be common, everything attached to mine is a BIG DEAL. When Birdman said, "put some respect on his name", this is what THEE symbolizes for me.

Aside from being a mom of two, I am a published author, content creator, and serial entrepreneur. I've been sharing my life behind the scenes and allowing everyone to get to know me personally on YouTube since 2020. I wanted everyone to know that I am a young mom who doesn't have life all figured out, but I also don't let trials and tribulations defeat me. On there, I show my come-up journey, as well as how I juggle wearing many hats.

Although I've been writing since elementary school where I won my first writing award from the Secretary of State, I've been a published author since 2019. I started out with my urban fiction series, *Love, Lies N' Betrayal,* and now adding self-help books to my portfolio. I've always had a dream of being an entrepreneur, having been inspired by my maternal grandfather. He owned a transportation service based out of Charleston, South Carolina and was well known across the U.S.

My dreams have always been bigger than my bank account, so when I got pregnant at sixteen and graduated high school a year early, I went to college immediately after for my associate's degree. I entered healthcare as a Certified Medical Assistant to bring in decent money to support myself, my young son, and my business dreams.

My first business endeavor was a clothing boutique in 2013. I had no clue on what the hell I was doing, of course, and I hardly made money, but I knew I still wanted to keep going. Even though the clothing boutique didn't work, I tried my hands in many industries thereafter, and I've learned a lot about business from the L's that I've taken. From poverty to achieving my first six figures in business, it's safe to say I'm the goat with this business -ish!

Yes, I am a successful entrepreneur, however it was not easy. The saying, "you have to fail to succeed" is the truth. I've had many business ventures that have failed, and some I gave up on because I got in my head instead of getting in my bag. Let's see, A clothing boutique back in 2013—FAILED! A natural skincare line back in 2014—I QUIT! A residential and commercial cleaning company in 2016—I LET GO! Now, the cleaning company was definitely a win. We saw profit just two months in and kept that going for a while. That was my first and most successful business before becoming a published author in 2019.

Business was boomin', employees were hired, and many lessons were learned. We were booked, busy and paid, *Okurr*! I'm talkin' five-figure months consistently only three months after launching. You're probably thinking, 'If it was all peaches and cream, Courtney, why the hell did you let it go?' Reason being was that's not where my heart was.

With choosing a business venture, it's not always about the money. If you get into business for the money, the business will never last. You must enjoy the work you do, to be enthusiastic about doing it.

The cleaning company was a steppingstone for where I wanted to be and what I actually wanted to do. Cleaning toilets and wiping baseboards was cool for a while, but if I was to do it all over again, I would be on the back line, and hire an entire crew to be on the frontline. That was my goal for that business. Instead, I decided to temporarily close that business and fund something I was more passionate about, which was writing.

I published my first novel in 2019 and have been publishing bomb-ass books ever since. So, do I regret the moves I made with the cleaning business? Hell naw! I was always passionate about writing and writing made me who I am today. So, choosing a business you're passionate about is so important—but when people are in business just to make money—they won't understand this. Yeah, the money will come, but for how long? How long will you really be in business if you hate what you're doing and you're not motivated enough on the daily to continue?

Throughout my years as a businesswoman, it was the perseverance in me, the passion, the determination to succeed, and the dedication of breaking generational curses that kept me going no matter what. For many, the prize is the ability to flex with designer and brag on having "a business." For me, it's the ability to provide a life for my family and kids that I didn't have and build an empire for my legacy to continue when I'm gone. To be honest, my main goal for entrepreneurship is about helping others, building a community, and being a relatable example that the struggles you experience and your circumstances does not limit the heights you can reach when you work hard and have faith.

The ultimate goal in business is increasing brand awareness and to obviously get to a point where your business is generating consistent sales even when you ain't doing 'ish. If you do this right, brand awareness will lead to more followers, higher engagement rates, and increase sales.

The reality of this is, only 10% of startup businesses succeed, and of course the other 90% don't. About 10% of that ninety fail within the first year. Simply because of lack of knowledge in their industry, lack of knowledge on how to scale and run a business, lack of funds to keep investing, ineffective marketing, partnering with the wrong people, entering the wrong market, and not managing their business income properly. Don't get discouraged, though. A big part of business is research and knowledge. Have you heard the saying, "when you know better, you'll do better?" It pertains to a lot of things in life, especially entrepreneurship. Luckily for you, I'm gonna set you up for success by covering all those topics in this book. Now what you do with this tea is all on you!

2

Get Yo' Life Sis

First, I want to start by congratulating you on this major step in your life. Whether you're a new or aspiring entrepreneur, you deserve praise.

As you may know, starting a business can be intimidating, and entrepreneurship isn't easy, but the fact that you are still willing to follow your dreams is already a huge accomplishment within itself.

This book is loaded with information because of course, my goal is to help you become or grow into a successful business owner, but just take it one step at a time. This isn't one of those books you read and toss afterwards. But instead, kept close to you to serve as a resource guide for you from here on out. I'm gonna give you the tea on this business 'ish as promised, but you still must be willing to apply, work hard as hell, be consistent like a mother—, and be prepared to stand alone if you have to. It's important to have business relationships with others (which I will talk more about this later), but there will be times when you will have to put your big girl panties on, wipe your own tears, and figure this shit out by yourself. I want you to be prepared for that.

Be Authentic

I've always enjoyed watching successful and upcoming entrepreneurs talk about their journey and what they've done to get where they are. Especially the folks that I can relate to. The ones who grew up in poverty, been raised by single moms, experienced life living in the hood, who became teen moms, and anyone else who may have had all odds stacked against them, but still came out on top. It allows me to keep faith, inspires and motivates me to be bigger and do even more.

I've watched interviews with Jayda Wayda, Lil Baby, Coi Leroy, Tyler Perry, and Issa Rae. I've watched influencers like Ari Fletcher, B.Simone, and De'arra. They are doing their own thing and have gotten a taste of success at different times of their lives, in different ways. What I noticed when listening to their success journeys was that they all mentioned authenticity, and how they stayed true to who they are.

I am me 1000%, no matter what. When you are, some people will like it, and others won't. You have to understand that your personality isn't for everyone, but that shouldn't stop you from being your authentic self. It wasn't until a few years ago that I realized this for myself. I was such a people-pleaser. I wanted everyone to like my YouTube videos, so I tried talking properly. I didn't want people to label me as jokey, so I stayed quiet at events and around certain people. I was scared to release my romance fiction novels because I didn't want people to think I was weird for the type of stuff I came up with in my head. Then, I finally stopped giving a fuck, accepted it for what it was, and became true to myself.

I started acting my normal self. Mostly, when I got around people, they would tell me I'm a vibe. For the people that didn't like my personality, well, they got distance and two middle fingers on my way out. I started being myself on YouTube, and viewers commented on my channel all the time about how real I was and how much they loved that. For those books I was scared to release, well I found my balls. When I did, it created a huge fan base and loving community, and made me six figures in my first twelve months.

When people feel purity and realness, they flock to you. Your support will flow naturally. Why? Because it's rare to see that these days. So, you decide, are you going to share your unique personality with the world, or are you going to imitate someone who already exist and fail while doing so?

With social media, music, and society, these days it's very easy to unknowingly get caught up in the mix of imitation. However, when you are your authentic self, people will eventually like you for who you are, what you do, and what you're not. It's going to be easier to move when you're moving genuinely. Trying to be who others want you to be will always take more energy than what it takes for you to be yourself. Besides, it'll be less stressful. Remember who you are and stay true to that. It's all about being confident in who you are and having a clear mind when elevating.

Clear your mind

Writing has always been a passion of mine since I was a little girl. I used to write the lyrics to my favorite song, write stories I made up, and as I got older, I started writing in a diary. The diary was where I kept my thoughts, feelings, my little school crushes, and that's all I can remember about that. What I'll always remember about those times or any time in my life was how much writing healed me. I know this may sound crazy, but a piece of paper and a writing utensil was my therapy for a long time. Way before I knew professional therapist existed.

Growing up, I was a very sensitive kid, and I felt like I didn't have anyone to talk to. I hardly had friends for whatever reason. I'm the only girl and the oldest of three, so I wasn't getting the most attention. My mother was, and still is, nonchalant about everything, so she never took me seriously or was very understanding. For the others in my family, talking about how I felt was nerve-wracking being that open discussions weren't a normal thing for us. Now you see why paper and a pen were so important to me. If I didn't have that, I would've probably turned out to be a fucked-up individual.

In many families, this has been the reality for generations. It's hard to blame my mom for being who she is because that's what she's been taught. Remember, it only takes one person to make change and create better habits. Why not let it start with you?

Believe it or not, your childhood trauma and experiences follow you into your adult life. If you go through life without acknowledging the problem and dealing with it head-on, it will reflect in the way you treat people, the way you talk to folks, the way you view life itself, the energy you give, and your performance. You can't allow the fucked-up things or people you've dealt with in the past, control the way you live presently. You, the genuine people around you, and your dreams don't deserve that.

For me, meditation, journaling, praying, and positive affirmations are the go-to secret recipe for not only a clear and healthy mind, but also for being a successful entrepreneur. Increasing your vibration with healthy daily habits is extremely important. You won't be in the mood to do what you need to unless you're in the right head space to do so. You must train your mind every day to think positively no matter what is not going right for you at the moment. Instead of being in your feelings about what's not going right in your business, figure out a game plan on how you will get the shit you need to get done, done. Instead of saying, "I think I made a mistake on starting this business", say, "I'm built for this, I got this." Instead of quitting, take a quick break to fuel back up. You wouldn't leave your car on the side of the road forever if you ran out of gas once, would you? Alright then, keep that same energy when it comes down to this business, sis. Yeah, I'm coming for you. You ain't finna quit on your dreams, not on my watch!

This is the type of mentality you have to refrain from, to not fall victim of that 90% failed business rate. Therefore, I stress how important it is for you to be mentally prepared and in the right headspace to embark on this wild journey. Your success is riding on that 1000%. The way we go about our day is based on how we feel. You must wake up, pray (to whoever you choose), speak life into yourself and your business, eat a healthy breakfast, read a mind-stimulating book, and listen to motivational words **EVERY SINGLE DAY.** The power of the tongue is real girl. I'm a witness.

I am obsessed with listening to Steve Harvey's motivational speeches on YouTube and to this podcast called *Slay Girl, Slay.* I also journal in my *"Get out yo' Head, Manifestation journal,"* (check my website for yours), repeat positive affirmations to myself in the mirror every morning, and do a five-to-ten-minute meditation daily. I make it my business to implement this into my schedule and get it done before I start any work. When I tell you these changed my life, it's true, I can't make this up.

I know it sounds like a lot, but you must get into a routine and make it a part of your day. When you enjoy what you are doing and see progress from it, it won't feel like a burden, but more of a necessary habit to create. You don't need to follow my routine or anyone else's. Figure out what works for you through trial and error, then make your own routine. It's going to take some time to figure out what works for you and how you want to go about doing it. That's ok. It's definitely a process, but like everything else in these entrepreneurial streets, stay patient and keep going.

I know many people don't understand meditation and I didn't either until I did some research and tried it out myself. Meditation does not have to be sitting down with the soles of your feet touching one another, humming, with your eyes closed in a quiet room. However, if that works for you, by all means, do it.

When I meditate, I like to be in a comfortable position and a quiet room. I simply repeat one positive affirmation over and over and over in my mind while breathing in and out slowly after each phrase. That's my meditation, and that's what works for me, but everyone is different. Find what works for you and take the steps to clear your mind and create peace in your life.

Protect your Peace

Now I know for minorities and in the black community, we are all determined to bring everybody with us as we reach our goals and elevate in life. That's not a bad idea, but you must come to reality and realize that everybody will not come to the top with you. For you to be your best self, you'll need to leave others behind that mean you no good. Understand that everyone who says they're for you, ain't for you sis. Many people are in your life just to keep up with it or reap the benefits of your hard work and success. Frankly, that's a form of negative vibration and energy that you do not need around you.

I know what it's like to want to help everybody, but you can't. You must think about yourself first. Especially when you're running a business and trying to build a six-figure one from the ground up.

Let me make it clear, it's not always friends that aren't genuine. Think about that cousin who's low-key hating on you and rolling their eyes every time you talk. Think about that auntie who down-talks your dreams. Or that uncle that's telling you to go get a nine-to-five job because you have bills to pay, and you don't have time to gamble on a business. What about that friend who constantly calls you to gossip about what she saw on Facebook or *The Shade Room's* Instagram page? Think about that cousin who says she wants to see you win, but anytime she can support you, she doesn't. I'm here to tell you that family can be just as draining as a bad friend. So, no matter how you feel about anyone or what their title is in your life, if they are not helping you elevate, they are hindering your growth for success. Oh honey, I would know.

I had this friend since middle school. We were click-tight. That was my girl. But, as we grew older, we lost touch. I became a mom at seventeen, and at that age, she was kid-free living her "best life." She had her other set of friends that she partied with and talked to most of the time. Meanwhile, I was raising a baby and trying to figure out life. I had responsibilities, she didn't. Fast forward to about four to five years later, we crossed paths and linked up again. Now, I'm the type of friend that goes above and beyond for my girls. If you need me, I'm there. If you're calling me all times of the night, I'll answer. If you're going through your 'ish, I'll tilt my shoulder for you. Everything was good for about the first year or two of us linking back up. That was until I got more goal-oriented, I shifted my focus on leveling up and wanted to secure the bag more than I wanted to dig into it.

She would call and text me all the time. She seemed to be excited about us gossiping and going out, more than she was when we talked about starting a business together. I love everything business. I always encouraged others to start one. I'm a firm believer that business owning is the key to generational wealth. So, when my best friend since middle school told me she wanted to sell lashes, I got excited. I thought this was a new her. She'd finally realized there was more to life than working a nine-to-five and living paycheck to paycheck. But every time I would ask her how that business was coming along; she would brush it off. Every time I would tell her let's link to write our business goals and our plans to achieve them, she would flake. The same energy she gave when it was time to go out and get drunk wasn't the same energy she gave when it was time to do something positive.

She would be drunk in the middle of the day. She would go out almost every night, and she'd even ask me to borrow money when she knew I had far more responsibilities than she did. But that wasn't what turned me away from her for good. It wasn't until I sat down and thought about the type of relationship we had. When I needed her, she wasn't there. When I called her, she hardly answered. That's when I realized I was overplaying my part in her life and was more of a friend to her than she was to me. I was pouring into her, but I had nobody pouring back into me. It was draining.

With everything else that had happened, that was the icing on the cake. Long story short, she stopped answering my calls, and I stopped reaching out. We never talked about it and to this day, we haven't spoken.

Now, I can honestly say that the relationship her and I had meant a lot to me. I imagined us taking pictures on private jets together, showing the world who we are from 2006 to 2032 together, our kids calling each other cousins, us starting businesses together; us living in big-ass houses with matching Benz and so much more. But honestly, I wanted more for her than she wanted for herself, and I couldn't afford to carry that burden. Clearly it was my dream for that and not hers. But I was to a point in my life where I only wanted to be around people who hyped me up to be my best self and show up for me as much as I showed up for them. With that being said, I let that friendship go. I found myself saying, *'it is what it is,'* when it came to her. I guess it wasn't meant for her to go to the top with me, and I'm fine with that, too. I'd worked too hard to elevate to let anyone bring me down.

Another person was my dad. Since I can remember, he would show up in my life when he wanted to, then toss me like a cigarette bud when he was done being a parent, to me at least. He was always inconsistent in my life. Throughout the years, I tried several times to build a bond and better our relationship, but it was always the back and forth. One minute he was there, the next minute he was Casper the ghost. It was very inconsiderate of him, and toxic. Again, when I got goal-oriented and got more serious about protecting my peace, I cut his ass off for good, too. Let me tell you, when you can identify that the person who gave life to you doesn't mean you any good and can cut them off with no regret, you're a bad motherfucker. I turned him loose. He stopped reaching out and so did I. I finally blocked his number and went on with my life.

A few years after I became a published author, opened businesses, and started YouTube, this fool called my phone. *Wait a minute, isn't he blocked?* He was, but his girlfriend wasn't. *Damn!* I thought to myself.

The moment they realized they could reach me through her phone, I would get a call from them out the blue every time I was at my highest point in life. It seemed like those were my testing seasons. The devil was trying to steal my joy because anytime I spoke to him or about him, it would upset me. That's how I knew that the relationship needed to be demolished permanently. His presence disturbed my spirit, and I wasn't gonna make myself be ok with that just because he was *"my dad."*

Let me tell you how much protecting my peace to be my best self means to me. I spoke my peace to him for the last and final time at the beginning of 2022. Afterwards, I blocked his girlfriend's number too (now both of them are on the block list). I went to therapy and I no longer let that situation move me. I know I'm much better without him because I wrote this whole damn paragraph without dropping a single tear. Whew, if that ain't growth, baby I don't know what is.

Everyone you have around you or in your circle should be genuinely here for you and not what you have to offer them. The folks in your circle know your worth. Anybody around you should be able to offer you just as much as you can offer them, if not more. It doesn't have to be financially or materialistically either. Uplifting you and encouraging you to do better. Anytime you are sad or get hard on yourself, they remind you that you're that bitch and you got this. Those are ways that someone who wants to see you win can show you. Unfortunately, every person you are around won't have that type of mindset. It's up to you to be able to identify the people who don't, and act accordingly. That goes for relatives, business partners, relationship partners, and friends. The best decision to make is always the hardest one. Just because it's hard, don't let it stop you from doing what's best for you. I promise baby girl, you got this.

Negative energy is anything or anyone who brings down your aura, redirects your focus, or disturbs your spirit when they are around. People who talk down on your dreams, gossip about things that do not help you elevate, constantly take, and hardly give, has to go. It doesn't have to be money they take; it can be your time and knowledge as well. Those are leeches. They will suck you dry if you allow them to stay. Don't allow negativity to control your mind and take over your life. The earlier you deal with it, the better. Because no matter how much you elevate in life personally and financially, if you still have the negative vibes around you or the leeches sucking you dry, you will never be happy or able to live a peaceful life. At this very moment, we are saying bye to the dream killers, releasing dead weight and toxic energy.

You need motivators, inspirators and people who are mutually beneficial to you. Each person in your corner will serve a different purpose in your life. Know what their purpose is, and make sure it's worth having them around.

Having a mentor and hanging around other entrepreneurs is necessary. Hanging around other like-minded people can help keep you on your toes. It'll help with what you need to do to become your best self and be as successful as possible. Being around like-minded people builds a solid foundation and tight relationship because they understand the struggles you face as an entrepreneur, what you deal with on a day-to-day basis, you both are beneficial to each other, and can give valuable feedback to one another.

When you're hanging with people who are more successful than you, it will serve as motivation to keep your head in the game when things get tough. When I hang with other entrepreneurs or content creators, I call them silent mentors because having them motivate, be understanding, and inspire gives mentor energy without them even knowing.

A mentor doesn't have to be someone you can FaceTime or call. It can be a good book, movie, or podcast. A good mentor will keep it real with you no matter what and be open to sharing their failures along with their success journey. Keep in mind if a mentor say they've never failed, that's cool and all (which I highly doubt), but because they haven't, you won't be able to learn from their mistakes.

Building business relationships with legal and professional individuals is important as well. A healthy business relationship is having a designated bookkeeper who understands your needs and understands the way you operate your business. They know your weak and strong points and help you more in those weak areas. You need someone who holds you accountable and stays on top of their tasks and duties. Someone you can work side by side with to make sure things are getting done properly, and they be cool with your input or feedback. Someone you can call on anytime of the day and they are willing to help. Those qualifications apply not only to a bookkeeper, here are a few others you should build a good relationship with: an accountant, an insurance agent if needed, graphic designers, a business coach, a law firm, an assistant, and a social media manager, just to name a few.

Here's what they each handle:

- An **Accountant** keeps track of all the money. The revenue, the expenses, the taxes, the budgeting, etc. An accountant makes understanding your monies and filing taxes easier.
- An **insurance agent** takes care of your brick-and-mortar insurance and insurance for your employees. (This may not apply to your business needs).
- **Graphic designers** take care of all things graphic for your website, flyers, social media posts, etc. If you're not creative enough to design

these yourself or don't have the time, hire a graphic designer who delivers what you need and is dependable enough to get it done on time. Having one to two you can rely on is a great start.

· A **business coach** is someone who leads you down the right path to business success. This is someone who can help you when you reach a roadblock and someone who holds you accountable to get things done.

· A **law firm** should be a law firm and not a specific lawyer. You want a law firm that contains lawyers that practice different laws such as: intellectual property laws, contract law, employment law, formation law, and business lawsuits. Intellectual law pertains to trademarks, logos, copyrights, patents, etc. Contract law pertains to reviewing and creating contracts and handles business negotiations. Employment law is for handling discrimination concerns, wages, sexual harassment issues, etc. Formation law is for handling legal entity creation for startup businesses. Business lawsuits is if your company is sued for anything or if you need to sue someone else pertaining to your business. Working with one good law firm versus several law firms is more professional and would be much easier to keep up with. Some law firms may refuse your service if you are working with competitors, anyway.

Mind yo' Business

Have you ever seen a meme on social media that says, *"mind the business that pays you?"* When you are running a business or starting one, it is critical that you stay focused.

One of the hardest things about being an entrepreneur is that you oversee your success. Unlike a nine-to-five, you're not being micromanaged to stay on task, or constantly being told to make sure you get yo' work done on time. You are the head honcho in charge. That's cool, but you must have it in you to be on time, to show up for your business, to get your work done, stay on top of marketing trends, and stay focused when you're working. That's naming a few things that come with this territory.

Let me tell you, that is one of the hardest things you will encounter because getting distracted is much easier than being focused and staying on task. You get so used to being the boss that it's so easy to become a procrastinator. "Oh, I'll do that tomorrow." Do not be that person.

When I became a full-time entrepreneur back in 2019, one of the hardest things for me was staying focused. I would sit at my desk, on my computer, with my phone right next to me. I'd make a list the night before of all the things that I needed to get done, but then I'd find myself on social media checking shit that had nothing to do with my business. I can honestly say that it wasn't on purpose, it was just a bad habit.

What helped me focus was planning out my day hour by hour. I wrote and prioritized my daily goals, blocked out times on the schedule for myself and my mom duties, and filled my tasks in on my schedule where I best saw fit.

I found that to be extremely helpful because it allowed me to accomplish as much as I could, but still not overwork myself. Whatever couldn't fit into my schedule during my hours of work, I left for the next day. Before I started this time management system, I'd be up at two in the morning making sure I got things done. I hated starting a task and stopping in the middle, so I'd be up all day, skipping meals even, because I was focused on getting my task completed. I am very goal-oriented, so accomplishing what I set out to do is a must for me. But, taking care of yourself and making sure you get an efficient amount of sleep is just as important.

Know what you want

Have you ever sat down and thought about the life you wanna have, the type of person you want to be, your dream storefront, or a city you'd rather be in? If you haven't, it's cool, for now at least. If you have, you are ahead of the game. Not everyone has their life mapped out or even knows what direction they want to take, and that's OK. If you know you want better and you're willing to work for it, you're on the right track. But it is also very important to know exactly what you want to work towards.

Since I was a little girl, I have always known exactly what I wanted in life. I wanted to be a writer since the first grade. When I was about twelve years old, I said I wanted to work in the medical field. At about age sixteen or seventeen, I was still trying to figure out and decide what I wanted to do. But by age nineteen, I knew I wanted to be an entrepreneur. I knew I wanted all these things, but my problem was I didn't know what kind of writer I wanted to be, what I wanted to do in the medical field, or what type of business I would open and be successful with. I knew what I wanted, but I didn't have it all figured out. If you are someone who doesn't have a clue about what direction you want to take or what you want in life, I'm here to help you figure it out. And we're gonna get this figured out right now because you can't set goals until you know what you want.

First, you must decide where your heart is. So, grab a piece of scrap paper, and I want you to write five things that you love to do. Secondly, I want you to make a little star next to your top three favorites, and they do not have to relate to one another. Then out of those three main favorite items that you starred, jot down a few businesses that could relate to each of the three topics. So, for instance, if my number one choice was that I like to do hair, I could jot down for that topic: braiding, wig installs, wig making, hair classes, salon. If my second topic was cleaning, I could jot down cars, houses, businesses, and yards. Lastly, if one of my topics was that I love being with kids, I could jot down daycare, babysitting, and teaching.

Now I want you to pull out your phone. We just talked about staying focused, so I only want you to pull out your phone for one reason, to do some research. Research is big in business, so you might as well get used to it. I want you to go to Google and type in, "How much does it cost to start a ... business?" Once you find that out, write that next to the first topic and repeat for each of them until you are done.

So now, we have figured out what you like to do and how much these potential businesses will cost to start. You need to figure out how much money you can afford to spend on this new business. If you know your taxes are about to drop and you're getting eight grand, ask yourself, "Can I afford to invest this whole eight? Or do I only have three out of the eight to touch?" If you do not want to use your own money, decide if you are willing to take out a loan, use credit cards, or try for a business grant (more on funding your business later). You'll have to dig into your finances and decide what will be the best option, without hurting your day-to-day living. I can't tell you what to invest. Assuming you have figured that out, we are going to move on to the next step. Circle the topics that are in your budget. Whichever you cannot afford now, you can't do it. But that does not mean this is a forever decision, it just means you will need to work a little harder and more strategically to come up with the money for the others. It is important to know the startup cost of a particular business and how soon those types of businesses turn a profit.

I saw a quote and I love this quote dearly. It said, "failing to plan, is planning to fail." Write that on a sticky note and stick that on your mirror because you need to be reminded of this every single day. This applies not only in the entrepreneurial life, but to your personal life. Be smart about the decisions you make and make sure you are prepared to do your best. If you are not planning ahead of time and are just winging it 99% of the time, then you will not be successful.

Be clear on what you want, ask the universe for it, make a game plan to get it, and don't stop until you do. Even when you have achieved all the goals that you have set for yourself, create new ones that challenge you even more. You should always choose to be better and do better than what you have already done. Trust the process and be grateful for what's given to you along the journey whether it's good or bad.

The decisions you make should be made after strategic planning. If you're going to be a CEO, make sure you think and move like one. Remember, you are the boss. Stand on that. Don't let anyone tell you what to do in your business! Don't let anyone choose your path for you because of what they see someone else doing. An important thing to also remember is, never compare your journey to others.

Creating a Millionaire Mindset

Success starts with your mindset. You must first know that you will succeed before you can, and have positive thinking. Not having the proper mindset can have a negative impact, which can be draining. If you're not happy, it will reflect in the work you do.

You must believe in yourself and be willing to take all steps necessary to achieve what you set to accomplish. Shortcuts are a no-no and handouts won't get you but so far.

You must learn constantly. Invest in yourself as much as you can. Enroll in those classes from trusted individuals. Buy those books you've been looking at that will teach you what you need to know and use the internet as much as possible. The resources are there, use them.

Don't be afraid to fail or take a risk. Failure isn't bad, it's necessary for success. Learn to shift a failure into a lesson. Turn negativity into something positive by learning from your fuckups and growing from your mistakes. Just make sure to not make the same mistake twice.

Work hard for you and your business. Work hard to evolve into a more positive person. Work hard on implementing that meditation and book reading into your schedule. Work hard on creating healthy habits. Work hard on your campaigns and marketing strategies. Work hard on dissecting your analytics. Baby, just make sure you don't play when it comes to you and your business. Always give 150%.

Stay focused. Put that phone down after you've scheduled that content. Don't click on *The Shade Room* post if it ain't speaking elevation or growth opportunities. When you run into tough decisions and times get hard, remember that it won't last. This time may be hard, but once you figure it out, the next time won't be. When you feel like quitting, remember why you started. When you see the amount of money you've spent on your business, don't complain. Be grateful that you can cover those expenses.

Stay organized. Keep your shit together. Your personal life may be in shambles, but your business doesn't have to be. Plan, plan, plan. Stick to the schedule. Keep track of your inventory in a software program. Use a booking app so you know what's going on. Keep your expense receipts in binders. Girl, keeping the business clean and cutthroat is just as important as keeping your lady parts clean. If you are slipping on the cleanliness of your business, I'm gonna assume you're slipping on your hygiene, too. I'm jus sayin'.

There's one book that I read repeatedly. Only because the author is dope, real, and entertaining. I got a chance to vlog with him, and he is cool as fuck. He is one of my inspirations, and I pray I get to work with him one day. It's 50 Cent. His book "Hustle Harder, Hustle Smarter" is a damn-good book. When it comes to elevation and creating that millionaire mindset, I would recommend reading this.

As I read it, it gave me the confirmation I needed, and that's what I liked. He mentioned how you can't develop the hustle; it has to already be in you. Seriously, you must have that boss mentality to succeed in this competitive-ass world. He mentioned how he never let failure defeat him. How important it is to have a solid team and how every chance should be considered an opportunity. This is the true definition of having a millionaire mindset. Only true hustlers and dedicated millionaires will have this mindset and attitude. That's what I want you to understand.

I always tell people, it ain't about where you come from, it's about where you are going. If you make the effort to get more, you shall receive. When you face challenges or obstacles, work on overcoming them until you do. Everything you go through is a part of your journey. One day you'll be able to talk about it and inspire others.

Requirements to becoming a millionaire

1. **Be Fearless-** You can't be afraid of failure. Scared money don't make money. You must be willing to do what makes you uncomfortable and take risks. Always choose faith over fear.

2. **Be Ambitious-** You must have the desire to win. You must want success more than anyone else wants it for you.

3. **Be Persistent-** Keep trying and don't give up. Figure out what didn't work, adjust, and try again until you get what you desire.

4. **Be Dedicated-** Even if you don't feel like doing it, still get it done.

5. **Have Hustle-** Be willing to put in the work and go above and beyond to bring in the money, even if you're tired. You must work hard, and even when you're working hard, work harder.

6. **Be Consistent-** No matter if the outcome isn't what you expected, and even if you don't feel like it, keep doing it.

7. **Plan-** Know the direction you are going to take and the moves you will make before doing so.

8. **Have Knowledge-** Be on top of your niche. If you don't know something, research until you figure it out. No matter how much you know, keep learning.

9. **Take Action-** A plan doesn't matter if you don't put it in motion. You must do everything you need to do to achieve your goals.

10. **Have the Mindset-** Create and stick with positive thinking and the ability to do anything.

11. **Be Courageous-** Sometimes you must create the opportunities you desire. No question is dumb, not asking is. You will either get a yes or

no, but you must try, even if it makes you uncomfortable.

12. **Stay Focused-** There will be lots of distractions but keep your head in the game no matter what.

13. **Dream Big-** Never sell yourself short. Even if it seems unreal or impossible, it's still important to think big, go big, and talk big.

14. **Be Disciplined-** Figure out a routine that allows you to be as productive as you can and accomplish all that you need. Nothing else matters if you lack discipline. Without this, there's no way to be successful.

15. ***<u>DO EVERYTHING I TELL YOU TO DO IN THIS BOOK!</u>***

16. **After you're done with this book, cop part two.**

3

Basics in Business

When starting a new business, there are a few things you need to keep in mind and take care of before running down to get a business license, sales tax license, etc. I mean, how are you going to get a business license anyway if you haven't come up with a name yet and don't know if the desired name is available for use or not? How are you going to reach out to graphic designers for a bomb-ass logo when you don't know the colors that represent your brand? You're probably sitting on your couch reading this right now like, "damn, sis is right. I haven't thought about any of this." No worries girl, I'm gonna get you and your business together.

In this chapter, we will cover the basics in business.

· How to write a proper business plan
· Business funding
· Business resources
· Identifying target audience
· How to come up with a business name
· Figuring out your brand values
· How to identify your competition
· Setting up a legit business
· Choosing a business structure

· Building business credit
· Choosing website hosts
· Domains
· Professional emails
· Trademark/ Protecting your brand
· DBA (Doing Business As)
· Branding
· Setting measurable business goals
· How to measure business success

In business, you must always make sure that your ducks are in a row and that your ass is covered at all times. When your business starts growing, you will become more susceptible to IRS audits and becoming a target on competitors' radar. I don't want to scare you, but it's the reality of being a business owner. I know you've heard the saying, "More money, more problems."

It's always smart to be prepared and not need it, than to need it and not be prepared. Always run your business like a multi-million-dollar corporation from the day you set it up. I don't care if it's you alone on your team, or if your monthly business income is five dollars. Make sure the business is legal, you are on top of payments and paying taxes, your receipts are upkept, and so on and so forth. By the end of this chapter, you will know how to start a legit business. If you're established, you will know what you should have completed already as a legit business.

Business Plan

A business plan is the overview of your business as a whole. This includes your business goals, your plan to achieve those goals, and when you will achieve them. Lots of rookie business owners look past this, but every business should have one.

This formal document is required when getting business loans, business funding, and finding investors. Some business plans are more extensive than others. It depends on the type of business you have, how long you've been in business, and the goals you set out to achieve. This is the first step you should take when deciding to start a business. Your business plan should be completed before you spend a dime on the business. Every new business you open, or new location you open, should have a new business plan.

A standard business plan includes the following:
Section One is the business overview.
· The Name of the business
· Owners
· Business description
· Formation (Is it a sole proprietorship, single member or multi member limited liability company, a corporation, etc.)?
· Number of employees (if any)
· Location (e-commerce or location address)
· Industry (ex: fashion, technology, film, hair, nails, etc.)
· Mission statement (The goal for your business in two or three sentences)
· Brand values (what does your business stand on that set you apart? For example, Chick-fil-A is known for exceptional customer service, moving quickly, giving fairly fresh food, and saying, "my pleasure."

There's no other fast-food restaurant that does things like Chick-fil-A).

Section Two

· S.W.O.T analysis chart. To make this, draw a good-sized square, and divide it into four sections by adding a horizontal line across the middle and a vertical line down the center. Label the boxes strength, weakness, opportunities, and threats, putting one topic in each box. Then, make a list pertaining to each of the topics.

o **S**trengths- What does your business do or offer that makes you better than the competition?

o **W**eaknesses- What does your business struggle with?

o **O**pportunities- This pertains to your company and the industry as a whole. What is popping in the industry that you can jump on that resonates with your brand?

o **T**hreats- Who are new competitors approaching the industry? What internal problems do you have that will jeopardize business success and rapid growth?

Section Three should include industry research. This will give you an idea of what to expect in such an industry over the next few years. The industry growth projections will show how fast the industry is growing, if at all. You will be able to determine how many newcomers are entering it, why business owners leave or aren't successful, etc. This is where you become a P.I (private investigator), get nosey and dig deep. You need to know what's going on in the room before entering it. Going into something blindsided is a bad idea. If you can get the tea on what's going on beforehand, it can protect your business from failing and your bank account from crumbling. The info I stated above is a good starting point but the more you find out, the better. Grab those binoculars and get on it.

Section Four should include your goals for the business, in addition to how and when the goals will be achieved. Include a growth chart (in line chart or bar chart format) for a better visual of your goals.

When it comes to creating your business plan, remember, you can create this how you like. It does not have to be created in the order I mentioned. If they're more sections you'd like to add, do that. I wanted to make sure I helped you understand the basics and the bare minimum to include.

After the business plan is created, it should be looked at often, at least twice a month, to make sure you are on track to achieving your goals. The business plan serves as a road map for your business. It should be adjusted accordingly, as your business grows. Creating a business plan can be stressful, but it's necessary to have, even if you aren't looking for investors or a business loan right now. Take your time when doing your research and deciding on your business goals. Remember, you can adjust this as often as you'd like. It won't be perfect the first time, but the more you know about your business and the industry, the easier making adjustments to your business plan will become.

Business Funding & Resources

Most businesses get their startup capital from wealthy family members, money passed down to them, and bank loans. But if you came from the trenches and an impoverished family like I did, you must get it out the mud. Bank loans will be hard to get, and the only money you have is the one you work a nine to five for. I'm here to tell you that's ok. Back when I started, I didn't know about all the resources we have available to us as a small and/or woman-owned business. There are people out there giving grants (which means the money doesn't require payback) to these types of businesses. Some may look at it as a charity, but real bosses with millionaire mindsets will look at this as an opportunity. Humble yourself and tap in. These grants change often, so you'll have to search for them. A good place to find a list of business grants would be by searching Google and checking the SBA website.

There are several legit business grants out there, just take some time to find them. Use Google and study the organizations before providing them with any of your information. Steer far away from opportunities that sound "too good to be true," and anything that looks scam-ish. You do not have to take it out of your kids' mouths or try to flip that tax refund check every year to start your business. We have options.

When it comes to resources, there is Score and SBA. I love the SBA. It stands for the Small Business Association. This is a free program that offers guidance and assistance to entrepreneurs. They offer help to small, new, and established business owners. They do not discriminate. So, no matter what stage in business you're in, they can help you, and if they can't, they will direct you to someone who can. Google the offices in your area.

Business name

I found that naming your business can be extremely difficult. It might be hard to come up with something memorable and meaningful, then when you do, you may not be able to use it because someone else is. That's annoying and could be very discouraging. This often leads to people using their legal names, or random words that flow together, because the process has become exhausting.

When coming up with a business name, it should be simple, meaning-ful, and unique. You want something that's going to stand out. When people hear the name, their reaction should be, *that's different, but I love it.*

When coming up with a name, don't come up with one, come up with many. I would say three at a minimum. Remember, don't choose anything random. Think about the purpose of your business, what you sell or offer, and any inspiration behind starting the business. Always keep in mind that you don't want to limit yourself with the business name. It should be versatile enough to sell and offer other products or services in the future.

Using your legal name is the easiest route to take, but if you have a common name like me, it can cause a few problems along the way. If it's too common, it may not be eligible for protection through a trademark, or it may already be taken and unusable. Be careful when choosing your name and do tons of research online when you do come up with a few that you like.

Put the name in Google and see what pops up. Search for the domain and see if it's available for purchase. Put it in the search bars on all social media's and see what happens. My favorite thing to do is put it in the search bars on the SOS (Secretary of State) websites and the USPTO (United States Patent and Trademark Office) website. (FYI, there will be a lot of business terminology and abbreviations throughout this book. Make sure to cop my *'Talk Business to Me'* business terminology bible, so you can understand the lingo).

Once you come up with a name, hire a trademark attorney to do a due diligence on it. Even if you're not ready to pay for a trademark or go that route, still reach out to a trademark attorney as if you are, and get the search done. They will also dig deep to make sure your logo and name are available and can be trademarked in the United States. It will cost you, but it shouldn't be any more than $600.

I know that's hefty for just a search, but it's necessary. Imagine you starting this business and skipping this step. Now, you've started bringing in five to six-figure months, your business has caught the attention it needs, and you've spent thousands on a logo, storefront, sign, etc. Then you get a certified cease and desist letter that demands you to stop using the name and logo, or risk being sued! It's not worth it! You skipped out on spending $600 to make sure you're safe. Now you've lost a hundred grand on everything you've paid for because you can't use anything associated with that name. Whew...that made my heart skip a beat just writing that. That hurt me for you. Don't do it sis!

Target Audience

Your target audience are your customers or the customers you cater to and attract. This is huge and matters in these business streets because if you are spending tons of money on marketing and not showing it to the right people, you are definitely losing! Know who your audience is before spending a dime.

You need to sit down, think about what you have to offer, identify your customers, then define their needs. Create an avatar (customer analysis). Think about their age, their income, their jobs, their hangouts, their dislikes, what brands and businesses they spend most of their money with, if they have kids, if they're married or single, and where they live.

You should have a clear understanding now on how the product or service aligns with your customer needs. Instead of getting in your sister 'n law's business or worrying about Facebook friends who ain't tryna spend money with you, get in the business of your target audience so you can collect their coins.

Now your target audience can be multiple people, but they need to relate to one another. Target audience can change overtime but pick who you are targeting and talking to first. Once you've figured out who your target audience is, you can reach them by running ads, working with influencers, and blogs (more on reaching your audience in another chapter). Branding has the same concept.

Branding

Branding is how you want customers to perceive your brand. So, when branding, think about why you started the business. What existing brands and businesses do yours relate to? What is the message you want your potential customers to take from what you show? When developing your brand's tone, consider these things: How are you speaking? How do you get your point across?

Don't rush to develop the tone, it takes time to establish. However, as for any trial-and-error moment, take note of what worked and what didn't. Take in feedback and learn from it; that's the only way to elevate your brand.

Have you ever played guess the logo? That is a game on YouTube, and there is also an app for the phone. This is when popular brand logos are shown, but blurred, or maybe missing a few letters. It's created to see if you can recognize a brand logo from the small details and characteristics provided. It's crazy how so many people can recognize a brand even if the brand logo image isn't clear to the physical eye.

For example, if you see an orange bucket and the white letters are blurred, you automatically know that Home Depot is the brand. If you see a blue bucket and the white words are blurred, you automatically know it's Lowe's. If you see a yellow M, with a red background, you know it's McDonald's. If you see an Apple with a bite indentation on the side, you know it's an Apple product. I could go on and on about brand recognition and brand visuals, but I think you get the point. The same way we recognize these brands is the same recognition you want for yours. You want to be able to create that automatic identification for consumers for generations now and in the future.

Brand Visuals:

Visuals are the content you put out on social media, such as your logo design, your brand colors, and things of that nature. It should reflect the brand, build communities, share your mission, be engaging, and be great for campaigns. Always use the same style of branding, but with a new touch. Logos should be bold but quiet, never too loud. When designing your visuals, steer away from glitter, it's an absolute no-go. No character heads either. Your brand visuals should be relevant to the business, clean, and professional.

I hate to tell you, but detailed designs and fancy logos are out of style. Unless you want to immediately be identified as a rookie, stay far from using those types of logos. Logos should be trendy, sleek, modern, or nostalgic. Unless you have a vintage business of course. Your logo should be simple, but unique just like your brand name, and it should deliver a message. Don't get stressed coming up with a logo; do the best you can when deciding how you want it to look.

Many brands change their logos over time, as they should. You may not realize, but many of your favorite stores and brands had different logos than the ones you see and notice today: Nike, KFC, Starbucks, IKEA, and Adidas, just to name a few. When you get a chance, Google your favorite brands and store logo transformations over time. You'd be surprised what their first logo looked like. Their first logo may not have been the best, but it doesn't matter because they kept going. Don't get hung up on your logo design, make the necessary changes to it as your business grows, like they did. As a result of this, they're still standing, and their bank accounts are still growing. That's just a little tea on the logo history and why you shouldn't get so tied up on what you decide on now. Regardless, make sure it serves its purpose.

Brand image:

You need to know your mission and have a business plan before picking brand colors. Don't pick any color. It should have meaning, and it should resonate with your brand mission. Colors speak to the brain. Before deciding on colors and coming up with a logo idea, look at competitor's logos and brand colors. Knowing color-cycle psychology plays a big role in decision-making for your business and will work in your favor if used correctly.

Color psychology is the study of how people see something and how they react after seeing it. It has a visual and emotional impact, as colors set tones and vibes. Age and gender make a difference in how color psychology will influence someone. So, knowing your target audience is important. Are you noticing how this all ties together?

To give you an idea of how important it is, listen to this. Did you know that:

- *Red* represents strength, excitement, love, and boldness.
- *Green* represents health, luck, nature, and prosperity.
- *Blue* represents confidence, responsibility, idealism, and security.
- *Purple* represents mystery, wealth, royalty, and nobility.
- *Pink* represents femininity, emotion, love, and affection.
- *Orange* represents thoughts, ideas, creativity, and innovation.
- *Black* represents boldness, elegance, classic, and power.
- *White* represents purity, luxury, peace, and innocence.
- *Gray* represents professionalism, maturity, balance, and calmness.
- *Yellow* represents fun, cheerfulness, happiness, and hope.
- *Brown* is more natural and represents generosity and trust.

Think about the business whose tagline is, "We love to see you smile." Off the top of your head, you already know what business that is. (There goes brand recognition again). I say this to say, McDonald's chose their colors wisely and made sure their brand mission matched. Red also represents hunger. Studies have shown that when the eyes see the color red, it triggers hunger in the brain. Yellow represents happiness cheerful and fun. Every kid loves McDonald's, it makes them happy. Referring back to their tagline, the colors gave what it was supposed to give because McDonald's makes kids smile. This is what I mean when I say your brand visual, your brand message or mission statement, and your logo should all come together.

That's a quick rundown on the colors. If you think about big businesses today and the brands you love, their choice of color will make more sense to you.

Use Canva to create a brand board once you've gotten your logos done. Brand boards are used to help develop the look of your brand and give graphic designers a better understanding of your needs. A brand board includes:
- Main logo
- Alternate logo
- Submark/tagline
- Textures (if you desire)
- Brand colors with hex codes
- Inspiration pics that reflect your business or brand
- *Use Pinterest for inspiration*

Personal Branding:

Personal Branding is important for business owners and content creators. Personal branding allows you to build genuine connections, so your followers and customers can get to know you, trust you, and like you on a personal level, but don't force it. Authenticity is key for this to work.
- Show who you are, what you believe, and what you know.
- Share your story. What inspires you to be who you are and motivates you to do what you do?
- Uniqueness. What makes you one of a kind?
- Authenticity. What's the journey like? How did you get the outcome? Share the good and the bad.

Make your business legal

If you are serious about running a business, making it legitimate shows that. Otherwise, it's a hobby. Not only is it a good look to have your business fully legit, but it will save your ass from the government. The last thing you want to do is to be on the IRS's radar or get into a beef with Uncle Sam. If you do, that will be a battle you most likely will lose. He and his people do not play.

Making your business legit is beyond opening a bank account and getting a website. That's only the beginning. There are levels to this.

What you need to run a business will solely depend on your state because all state requirements are different, so be sure to double-check this. I will give you the rundown on the basics that the majority of us will need for e-commerce. That would include: an EIN, a DUNS number, a Business entity and/or DBA, a Business License, a Sales tax license, Articles of organization, a website, a bank account, and Trademark Protection.

First, start with an EIN because you'll need to put it on everything. EIN stands for an employee identification number. You may also see TIN (Taxpayer Identification Number), but they both are the same thing and are the same number. To simplify that, this is your business Social Security number. This is free to obtain by going to irs.gov. Your EIN will be used on your business bank accounts, when building business credit, and any legal documentation pertaining to your business. Although an EIN may not be required, it takes place of your personal SSN and helps separate your personal and business finances.

You will need to decide on a business structure. Will this business be a Sole Proprietorship, Limited Liability Company, Partnership, or Corporation? Take your time on deciding this and weigh out your options. Consider the pros and cons of having each, before choosing what will be more beneficial. Limited Liability Company also known as LLC is very popular, but that doesn't mean it is necessary for your particular business. If you do not need the added protection that comes with owning an LLC, then consider going with the sole proprietorship instead.

If you choose to do a sole proprietorship, you still can separate the business name from your legal name by using a DBA. For example, let's say Jessica Shanaye Brown has a sole proprietorship business for custom creations. She doesn't want her full name on the business documents and website, so she's doing business as Jessica Shanaye Customs. Later on in life, she decides she wants to add more under her "Jessica Shanaye" umbrella. She has added to her sole proprietorship that's a completely different business. Now she decided that Jessica Shanaye is also doing business as Jessica Wheels and Deals, selling cars and car accessories. Once you have opened one sole proprietorship business, you do not need to get another EIN for a different business name under the sole proprietorship umbrella. You will use the same EIN you originally got, but add to your DBA and have it refiled with the updates. Note that every time you add a name to the DBA and have it refiled, you will pay a fee. So, if you know you are starting several businesses that will need to be added. Try adding them all at once to save on the refiling fees.

So, to clarify, Jessica has separated her business name from her legal name. Although she cannot include LLC or Corporation behind her business name, sole proprietorship is still an entity. Separating her names with doing business as, still falls on her personally because the businesses are not separating her financially, with the protection an LLC and Corporation can provide.

FYI, LLC businesses can also get DBAs. DBA requirements vary city and county wise, so make sure you check with the city you are doing business in, to see if you need one. If you do, this can also be done on your Secretary of State website. The same place you would file for an LLC.

The pros and cons can be found online but make sure it's a trusted site that knows what they're talkin' about. I would recommend you go straight to the plug which is irs.gov. That way you know the information given to you is real.

Get a Certificate of Existence. It is the same as Articles of Organization. The Articles of Organization are what you will fill out to register your business in the state. The Certificate of Existence is what you receive once your registration is approved. However, this does not apply to you if your business entity is a sole proprietorship. You will not be able to receive this. To obtain this, go to *yourstate*.gov website. It is not 'yourstate.gov', but specifically *your state* website. For example., If you live in Alabama, visit Alabama.gov. The fee does vary depending on which state you are in. But in South Carolina, it was about one-hundred-fifty dollars to obtain.

Getting a retail license also known as sales tax license is necessary if you are selling physical products. It doesn't matter if you do not have a storefront. If you are selling on a website, you will still need a retail license to collect sales tax. Again, it may vary state to state, so just make sure you do a little more research on your specific state and check with your DOR (Department of Revenue) to see if your business requires a retail license.

For me, I needed a retail license in the state of South Carolina and when I moved, I needed one for North Carolina as well. It cost me about $50 in South Carolina and didn't cost anything in North Carolina. Again, you can visit your Department of Revenue office or their website to get this license. In South Carolina, sales tax isn't collected on services, so a retail license wasn't needed for my service-based business. With my product-based business though, it was a must.

You can get the business license at your City Hall in the city where you will be doing business. It does not matter if you have a service-based business, you still need one. This may not apply to you depending on your city and state, so just reach out to your City Hall wherever your business is located to see if you would need a business license.

In South Carolina, I've had both a service-based and product-based business and I have needed a business license for both. For my service-based business, South Carolina did not have one general business license for all cities. So, I had to get a business license for each city where I provided services. That meant I had about six business licenses I had to keep up with. Don't get me wrong, it was a headache, but not as big of a headache as I would have had if I didn't have it and had gotten caught.

When you're a startup company, it can be a pain dealing with the different licensing and requirements of running a business. Especially when you are taking care of these things on your own. But when you are well organized, it won't seem like so much and will be less of a hassle to keep up with. Not everything will be easy, but you must do what you need to to get where you want to be.

The price you pay for a business license depends on your estimated annual gross income. When first applying, of course you wouldn't have prior years taxes to determine your income, so for this first year only, you would need to estimate how much you would make to determine the fee. After that year, your fee per year to maintain your business license will depend on how much money you made the year prior, so it will vary. Whatever amount you report making is what your fee would depend on. I would aim for a smaller number when starting. You don't know how great your business will perform, and you can't afford to overpay on fees.

Business Credit

Get yourself A DUNS number. It's a nine-digit unique identifier for your business. It is used to access and identify businesses across the world. When building business credit or looking for a business loan/business credit card, a lot of banks search your business by your DUNS number to see your business credit history. It is not mandatory to have one, but if you feel like your business will benefit from having it, then make sure you apply at dnb.com.

When building business credit, there are free, quick, and easy companies to work with as well. Uline, Quill, and Amazon just to name a few. Companies with Net 30 accounts are also a place to start. Buy your business items using these accounts, then pay later. Once the company sends an invoice, you'll pay.

Over the years, I've built a strong business relationship with Uline. I love Uline because they have tons of products for many business types, and they ship quickly. Don't take advantage of this opportunity and ruin your relationship with such a wonderful business. Make sure you pay your invoices and pay them on time.

Trademarks, Copyrights, Patents

A lot of small businesses don't think it is necessary to obtain a trademark, copyright, or patent simply because they are a small business. I'm here to tell you, *it doesn't matter baby girl.* Sorry, there's no pity given to "small business owners." In fact, you are the one the bigger businesses come for when trying to steal ideas.

Don't get it confused, though. A trademark is used for the protection of an image, phrase, or name. A patent is for the protection of inventions. A copyright is the protection on literary work such as books, song lyrics, instrumentals, etc.

Every day, business owners are fighting for brands to stop copycats and counterfeits. Think about Christian Dior suing Porn star Gigi Dior over the name *Dior*. You know Dior has lawyers on deck along with paper (money), so they're good. Think about how the real Drake shut fake Drake down. No matter how many times they are tried, as long as they own that trademark, they will always win.

Now there are some celebrities and big businesses that have slipped on securing the trademark class and someone else came and slid it right from underneath their feet. Remember how Vh1 went behind Black Ink Caesars' back and trademarked Black Ink for the television and entertainment trademark category? What about Kanye versus Adidas about the Yeezy name and designs? People are shady, yes! But they also know it ain't theirs until it's theirs.

It's just as important to make sure you aren't using someone else's name or anything close to it. I'd hate for you to be in court as a defendant versus a plaintiff. If you ever go to court, you want to be the plaintiff. That's why I explained earlier in the chapter how important it is for you to hire a trademark attorney to perform an extensive search on your business name and logo design.

There is a big difference between being fully trademarked and being serious about a trademark without the registered protection. The R with the circle around it ® means that the symbol, tagline, or name is registered with the USPTO and ain't to be played with, PERIOD! The ®

symbol can only be used if it is registered.

The ™ behind a symbol, tagline, or name means that it is unregistered with the USPTO, but the creators are serious about it and if it is copied, legal actions will be taken. Although the logo or whatever isn't registered, if it's used by anyone other than the owners, the owner can still take the copycat user to court and demand them to stop using it. The ™ symbol can be used without being registered, as long as it's an original and is not infringing.

The © symbol is the same as the ® regarding meaning, but it's for copyrights instead of trademarks.

My trademark attorney works with celebrities and is very trusted and knowledgeable. She told me, it's recommended to use the ™ before registering with the USPTO for the ® symbol. Although it's highly recommended to trademark and easier to win a battle when it comes to your logo, phrases, and designs, trademarks aren't mandatory.

Your favorite brands are still using ™ behind their logos to this day. 3M, MacAfee, EA Sports, and Starbucks, just to name a few. They are big brands, marketing their logos without full trademark protection, and they are doing just fine. I wanted to bring it to your attention how you can still survive, without a fully trademarked logo right now. But the goal should be to eventually become fully protected.

Domains, Hosting, Emails

Get a domain that is not used. A domain is your website name, it looks like this – **www.TheeCourtneySimone.com**, sometimes like this https://blo g.theecourtneysimone.com, or **https://theecourtneysimone.com/busi ness**.

The *theecourtneysimone.com* is the domain, *https:* is the URL, */business* is the page, and *blog.* is a subdomain. When searching for an available domain name, all you need to type in is your desired domain, minus the .com or .org or whatever ending. You can search for this on GoDaddy.com. On GoDaddy, you can pick the ending you want once the available options are shown. Make sure to choose the completed domain you desire before checking out.

I love GoDaddy for this. That is always my go-to for my domains. I have used them for several years. More than seven years to be exact, and I have not had any issues. Their customer service is top-tier. I love how the website is easy to navigate. It integrates with any website host (the company that holds your e-commerce store information) without hassle. So honestly, I could only recommend GoDaddy because that's all I've ever used. I'm not saying that's the only option available, but I haven't dealt with anyone else to be able to vouch for them. This is just a recommendation, make your decision based upon how you feel.

GoDaddy also has specials for new domains. I have gotten a domain lasting two years for as little as $20 plus tax. That is an awesome price. But when buying your domain, I highly recommend you add domain protection to make sure your domain cannot be stolen and to provide privacy to the domain owner's address and name. I've always gotten protection on my domains because of these reasons.

Now for a website host, over the years I have had many. I have had Weebly, which I didn't like. It doesn't give your website what it needs to give. Unless you want limited growth opportunities and very basic designs, I would not recommend it.

I have also had GoDaddy, but I used it as a portfolio for my service-based business. It was ok and served its purpose for a reasonable price. I didn't need anything too upscale or fancy for a cleaning company. When it comes to selling products online, I'm not sure how great the GoDaddy website would be, but their prices are reasonable, I can say that.

I have had some experience with Wix. Wix is not a horrible website host. I can tell you that it's not as flexible and as good as Shopify though. Wix was very similar in price to Shopify, but it didn't have all the perks of adding a wide variety of apps to integrate into your website. If you can afford Wix but not Shopify, I would say adjust your budget in other areas and spend the few extra dollars to go with Shopify from the start.

This may sound like a foreign language to many of you who have not started designing or worked much with your online store yet. But, for those who have some experience with their online store and have a little experience as an entrepreneur, you may understand what I'm saying a bit more.

I've previously had a Wix store. I had it for about eight months. I paid for the entire website upfront for the whole year, vs. paying it monthly, which saved me some money. But, at my eighth-month mark, I decided that I wanted to switch to Shopify. I'd heard so many good things about Shopify. I liked how major companies used Shopify, and Shopify is the bomb, plain and simple. I wanted Shopify! I'm not saying that to hype them up. I'm not getting any commission or discounts by telling you this by the way. So, this is my honest review on Shopify. Switching from Wix to Shopify, was a pain in the ass. It got done, but it does require a lot of patience, back and forth, research, and money to get everything working properly. You would need to move your domain over as well.

When switching over, your customer information and previous orders will not be moved over completely. You would also need to redesign your website from scratch. Like I said, it's a pain in the ass. So that's why I tell you, go with Shopify from the gate so you can avoid all this B.S I went through. If I knew then what I know now, I would have said forget everything else and went with Shopify first.

So, when deciding on your website host, make sure that it's a website host you can see yourself using long-term because if you decide to change while running a business, you will have hell sis! Website hosts typically cost around $40-$50 a month depending on the level or options you choose at checkout. If you pay yearly instead of monthly, they all offer discounted rates. I do know that Shopify has some flexibility with monthly website pricing, but I'm not sure if that applies to new customers as well.

You must obtain a business email. If your website is fabulous-footwear.com, then your business email should be something like customerservice@fabulousfootwear.com. It should not be Tiffany23sexy@gmail.com. That gives rookie vibes and it's unprofessional and tacky. Make sure you purchase a professional business e-mail specifically for your business. It should match the domain name you've chosen. Do not use your makeup brand e-mail, for your footwear business. Got me?

I typically purchase my business e-mail through GoDaddy at the time of purchasing my domain, so when it's time to renew everything, it can all be done at the same time. I try not to deal with too many companies, so it's less hassle to keep up with. Business emails on GoDaddy range in price depending on your business needs, but it can be as cheap as $1.99 a month and that's not bad at all.

Business Banking

Make sure you open a business bank account for your business expenses and income only. This will help show the IRS that you are a real and serious business, and it helps keep your expenses and income in the same place. Just imagine having to go through all your personal bank statements to figure out what was business and what wasn't. Girl, it sounds ridiculous. Save yourself the headache and get yourself a business bank account. Having a business bank account also come with perks, depending on what bank you choose to go with.

Banks typically charge a one-time fee of about $30-$100 to open a business bank account. You also get a cute little business bank card with your name and your business name on it. It screams BOSS BITCH, OK?!

I know Wells Fargo, Navy Federal, Chase, and Truist all offer business accounts. But you could check with your personal bank and see if they offer business accounts as well. I'm sure they do, but just weigh out your options because sometimes going with your personal bank isn't the best move to make.

Setting goals

I can't stress enough how important it is to set goals; big or small. Setting business goals helps you and your team understand and optimize your marketing budget. With a product-based business, it can help you figure out and decide how much product you need to sell in a certain timeframe. With a service-based business, you can determine how many clients per tier of service you need and how many tiers you're selling in a month. It helps guide you in the direction you need to maintain a successful, money-generating business.

When setting goals, make them challenging, but realistic. Although they need to be achievable, go big and take action! Always break down your goals. Let's say your goal is to be a millionaire. Well, $1,000,000 a year is only:

- $83,333 a month
- $19,230 a week
- and $2739 a day

So, focus on making $2,739 a day to reach this goal. If you sell shoes for one-hundred dollars, you need to sell about twenty-eight pairs of shoes a day. If your goal is to make $2,739 a month, you need to make roughly $92 a day.

When starting, your numbers don't have to be high. Start with $1000 months and when you hit that, gradually increase.

- 1k/month = $34/day
- 2.5k/month = $84/day
- 6k/month = $200/day
- 10k/month = $334/day

That's based on a 30-day month. I also rounded up to the nearest dollar. Only because it's best to have extra than to come up short.

Using **S.M.A.R.T** goals is a great way to breakdown your goal setting.

· The **S** in SMART stands for specific. What's a specific goal you want to achieve? Is it to make money, get bookings, sell houses, gain followers, etc.? Who's in charge of making sure this gets done and what are the steps to accomplishing these goals?

· The **M** in SMART stands for Measurable. Make sure whatever growth performance you choose is measurable. Have a baseline so it can be measured over time. This includes numbers. How many do you need or what is the percentage increase you need, to reach the goal?

· The **A** in SMART stands for Attainable. How are you going to reach the numbers you need? After coming up with a plan, ask yourself, is this reasonable given my circumstances?

· The **R** in SMART stands for Relevant. The goal must be relevant to your brand mission and marketing strategy. Figure out why it's important to meet that goal, and what it will do for your brand if you do. Don't pull goals out of a hat, have a purpose.

· The **T** in SMART stands for Timely. Set a reasonable and achievable due date, but still make it challenging, so you have the desire to push and work hard for it.

In conclusion, this is what a SMART goal looks like when created properly:

The brainstorming example:

· **S**- Gain new readers by selling more part one of my Love, Lies, N' Betrayal book series. Marketing ideas are: consistent posting, email, and SMS marketing and one-minute video ad for Facebook and Instagram.

· **M**- Sell 1,000 copies of Love, Lies, N' Betrayal part one for June. We will measure sales on this particular product and the overall customer return rate.

·**A**– Run campaign ads on Facebook, and Instagram starting mid-May for June.

·**R**– This will bring in more revenue as readers who enjoy this book will also grab parts two and three without the need for marketing. This will create return customers and increase our customer return rate.

·**T**– Sell 1,000 copies by June 30, 2023.

The final result example:

Gain new readers by selling 1,000 copies of Love, Lies, N' Betrayal part one by June 30, 2023. This will be accomplished by running a short, one-minute book teaser video ad on Facebook and Instagram. We will target new customers with my targeted campaigns. The campaigns will begin running in mid-May 2023. To measure the growth performance, we will pay attention to the customer return rate, sales, and new reviews for this product. Because this series is a best-seller, with a returned customer rate of 95%, this will ultimately increase sales, bring new customers, and increase our customer return rate.

When you break down your goals, it doesn't seem so far-fetched. It seems easier to reach, and less stressful to think about. The sky is the limit. Whatever you want, or see for yourself, you can have. Don't let anyone tell you otherwise. Like I said before, you can't have a goal without direction, and knowing the direction is pointless if you ain't taking action. It all works together.

Measuring Analytics

Analytics are what is used to measure performance over a certain period. Analytics are available for social media platforms, websites, landing pages, email campaigns, ads, and more. Analytics will give you the information you need for direction. Although analytics can be exciting to see, sometimes it can break your heart too. No matter what feeling you get when it's time to check those numbers, it needs to be monitored regularly. You need to know how and when to pivot, what type of content to create more of, and what types of content to stay away from. If you're serious about your business growth, in your analytics is where you need to be. Remember, people lie, numbers don't.

There are certain metrics you should check based on your goal.

For brand awareness, look at the post shares, post reach, gained followers, engagement rates, website visits, ad reach, website store sessions, etc. These are called vanity metrics. This tells you how many people, and if the right audience was reached. It tells if they were new or returning, and how much they liked your content. These are also called vanity metrics.

Vanity metrics look good on paper, make you feel good, and are easy to see, but they aren't enough to help reach sales goals. Although these aren't metrics for sales goals, it is still important to review them.

For sale goals, look at conversion rates, e-mail CTR (click-through rates), e-mail sign-ups, website sales, and ad performance metrics.

Sales goals metrics require more work. It's more time consuming as you need to look into sales funnels (automation that requires a series of actions to reach a goal), but it's necessary for major business growth and to make sure money is being spent wisely. Iconosquare is a good app to get detailed analytics. It's my fav.

4

It's time to BOSS UP

You are making it sis; I know this is a lot of information to take in, but I'm only trying to set you up for success. I'm here with you. Take a deep breath, stand up and stretch a little, grab a fresh glass of water, hell even some wine. Whatever you need to do to continue. As we get further in the book, things will get a little more intense.

In this chapter, we will get more into the day-to-day business aspects of things. We will cover:
- Customer service & how to provide it exceptionally
- Pricing
- Determining profit margins
- Understanding the growth stages in business
- Hiring and managing employees.
- Intro to social media
- How to choose the most profitable social media platforms
- Content creation
- Content ideas

Customer Service

If there is one thing I hate most, it would be bad customer service. When someone chooses to shop or work with you instead of tons of other businesses offering the same thing, you should cherish that. Don't nobody have to come spend their money with you, and if you provide poor customer service, that will be their last time.

Providing your customers and clients with top tier service and an exceptional experience should be a priority. It starts with you. You are the face of the brand, and their expectations must be met by you first before you can expect anyone else on your team to do the same.

Customer Service is your customers' experience when interacting with your business. You should never make a customer feel like they are an inconvenience. Providing good customer service isn't just being polite, manner-able, helpful, and smiling; it's that, plus more. If they are purchasing digital products, provide deliverables in a timely manner. Ask for reviews after purchases to build trust. Optimize your website for desktop and mobile so their shopping experience is a breeze. Provide them with reliable products and services they can count on. If they have a complaint, remain kind, be an active listener, and solve their problems _immediately_. Check your e-mail in the morning and before leaving so your response time is good. Have policies in place and make them easily accessible, so there are no surprises. Prioritize your customer needs. Do what you promised them. It's important to keep in touch with them as well by sending emails and posting regularly on social media. You want to make sure you are keeping your business at the forefront of their minds.

By now, you should know how much I love Chick-fil-A, so I'm going to use them as an example. Let's compare Chick-fil-A to Zaxby's, only because their competitors. These two both sell chicken, but their customer service are on different levels.

It's obvious Chick-fil-A takes pride in their customer service; all of their staff are ALWAYS in a great mood, they make sure they ask if you need anything else before pulling from the drive thru window, they always greet you kindly, and before you leave, they make sure they say, "my pleasure." Do I need to mention how every time you go to Chick-fil-A, you can count on fresh food? Even if you do have an issue with your food quality, once it's brought to their attention, it's resolved immediately. They will replace your problem item and then some. What about them bringing your food to your table when dining in? I mean they really treat their people like royalty over there.

Now, let's go over to Zaxby's. Zaxby's has a wide variety to choose from and the food is good *sometimes.* That's about all I have to say about them. That's the honest truth. The negative with them are, there could be no line in the drive thru, but they still move slow and keep you waiting. Let's not talk about them pulling you up, to get you out their faces at the window and to keep you waiting longer. They seem to have an attitude no matter what, including the managers. If you dine in, they will stand behind the counter and yell your order until you come and get it. They hardly ever thank you for your service, I mean the list goes on.

This may seem petty to some, but these are the things that differentiate similar businesses from one another, and what plays a big part in customers decisions on where they will spend their money. I've heard many times people say they won't get into a certain business industry because "too many people are doing it." Quite frankly, that doesn't matter when the competitors aren't delivering the products and services like you can. Stand out, bring warmth and comfort to your customers, be kind, and they are guaranteed to choose you over others.

Based on Google, check out these stats when it comes to customer service.

· 77% of customers recommend a brand after having a good experience.

· 67% of businesses can be saved from bad talk from a customer if the issue is resolved the first time and resolved promptly.

· 56% of people turn away from companies where bad customer service was received.

· 66% of people believe good customer service is simply having a polite and helpful customer service representative or team member.

Now, let that sink in. It's an easy and a simple gesture to be kind and caring.

Pricing

Understanding pricing is extremely important. You don't want to overcharge your customers and run them away, but you also don't want to have your prices so low that you're selling yourself short. If you're not making any money (or barely making it), that defeats the purpose of being in business.

Of course, at the beginning, it's going to take a while to turn profit, but as time progress, you should be getting closer and closer to profit. If you're not, something ain't right. The rule of thumb to figure out a retail price is, the COG (Cost of goods) multiplied by three, but when starting out, only multiply by two, then compare your prices to your competitors'.

Understand that COG is not only what's paid to vendors for your product, but the final cost of making your products or services what it is, in order to sell it. Costs to include when calculating COG are the shipping, product cost, shipment packaging, website design, thank you cards, loyalty cards, tissue paper, labels, hangtags, printer paper, computer, merchant fees, hosting fees, marketing, equipment, contractors, software, shipping label printer, shipping labels, time, etc. just to name a few.

Depending on your business, it could be more to include in your COG, or it could be less. Any and everything you put into this product in getting it to the customer should be accounted for. Each product should have its own COG calculation. Every time you introduce a new product or service, COG should be calculated for that product or service. It's always advised that you use a spreadsheet to keep track of COG and product/services pricing.

After you've figured out the COG and suggested retail price, you can estimate your profit margins. To find your profit margins, you'll need to do some basic math.

Step 1:
  Total revenue – COGS ÷Total Revenue.

Step 2:
  The answer from step one ✖ 100.

Step 3:
  The answer from step two is the profit margin.

Profit margins tell how much you're actually making, and it should be calculated every time you adjust a price or put out a new product.

That is so you can determine if your pricing is reasonable for both you and the customer. Profit margins that are five percent are considered low, ten percent is considered standard, and twenty percent or above is considered high ("good", as long as product pricing isn't too high and scaring customers away).

If your products/services are high-end or considered luxury, your prices shouldn't be the only thing that reflect that. So should your customer service, shopping experience, quality, content, packaging, etc. There should always be reasoning behind your chosen price. Also have reasoning for price increases.

Let's compare Chick-fil-A to McDonald's for this. Although they sell different foods, they are both popular. We all know that Chick-fil-A is a little pricier than McDonald's. At Chick-fil-A, a chicken sandwich meal with a side and drink can be on average about $13 and at McDonald's about $10. What sets them apart is not only the pricing, but the experience and food quality as well. Chick-fil-A can charge $13 for a chicken meal and still keep their customers wrapped around the building. They can charge $13 without complaints because the customer service is top tier, and the quality is bomb. You can taste the love in every bite of Chick-fil-A food.

This is why most people would choose to spend that extra $3 there, versus going to McDonald's. You can choose to go to McDonald's to save $3, but the food may be cold, you may sit in the drive thru line for thirty minutes, the staff may be rude, your chicken sandwich may be sloppy, and the quality will be basic. If McDonald's starts charging Chick-fil-A prices without the extra love Chick-fil-A give, their customers would look at them crazy, even the loyal ones.

Typically, it's fair to start increasing your prices slowly after being in business for about two years. However, this is just advice, remember you are the boss and don't let anyone tell you what to do. If you feel like you need to increase prices before then to keep your head above water, and your doors open, you do just that. Don't let anyone tell you what your prices should be either. You also have the right to refrain from explaining your price increases as well.

The Five Growth Stages of Business

There are several stages of business. This isn't something that's talked about often, so I wanted to make sure I covered this. It will help you plan for the future, make more informed choices in your business, and prepare for later challenges. It gives you a clear understanding on what level of business you're at and encourages you to elevate. Knowing what business stage, you are in helps determine the managerial factors that you must deal with.

Here are a few reasons why it's important to know your business stage:

1. Factors change from one stage to another

2. As the business grows, you'll know when and who to hire.

3. At certain stages, owners will spend less time doing and more time managing.

4. Get an understanding of cash changes as the business changes. In early stages, solid vendor sources, customer relations, exposure, etc. is critical to success. In later stages, losses are more easily compensated for.

5. To ensure you aren't holding on to fatal strategies. For example, delaying tax payments isn't as serious in stage one as it is in stage five.

6. So, you're able to recognize and deal with the heavy financial, time, and the energy demands of a new business. (This is irrelevant for stage two because the common problems has been bypassed or resolved).

<u>Stage One:</u> **Existence**- This will be a newly started business.

In this stage, the main problem is obtaining customers, and the owner does everything.

o Systems and formal planning are either inconsistent or nonexistent.

o The goal for these businesses is to stay alive and running. If growth is a struggle, these business owners will typically close the business when capital runs out.

o These entrepreneurs get worn out quickly and tend to quit faster.

<u>Stage Two:</u> **Survival**- This is a more established business.

In this stage, the main problems are that business owners struggle to break even or struggle to generate enough money. This stage of business has limited employees, and staff are supervised by general or sales manager.

o Systems are in place, but not many.

o The goal for these businesses is to make it through. Business can grow and profit but may remain at this stage for a while. These businesses can be sold but may take a loss.

o These entrepreneurs either retire or quit.

<u>Stage Three:</u> **Success**- This is a business that is profitable and has the ability to expand. In this stage, the main problems are growth and role decisions. The business owners must decide whether they will expand or keep the company stable and profitable. Owners decide if they will stay or disengage from the company. These are difficult decisions for the business owner to make at this stage. Typically, the owner steps back and has managers in place.

o Systems are typically in place and followed.

o The goal is for the owner to eventually part ways and step back to avoid a cash drain. Can it continue as it is with success, be sold, expand, or merged at a profit?

o Franchise becomes an option at this stage in business.

Stage Four: **Takeoff**- This is a business that's profitable, and for the most part always breaks even. At this stage growth decisions are critical. In this stage, the main problem is how to grow rapidly and how to finance the growth. The original owner is typically replaced voluntarily or involuntarily by investors or creditors.

o Systems are typically in place and enforced.

o The goal is to grow and not jeopardize the business profitability in the process.

o If expansion isn't possible, it is safe for the business to stay at this stage or go back to stage three, because growth is too expensive. They can even back down to stage two but must be careful because making that move can potentially cause failure. It depends on the growth decision.

Stage Five: **Maturity**- This is a business that's well-structured and fully profitable. In this stage, the main problems are controlling financial gains brought by rapid growth, expanding team fast enough to keep up with produced growth, and professionalizing the company. At this stage there is a huge team of employees, managers, and financial resources.

o Systems are professionalized and upgraded without changing the business quality. Systems are extensive and well developed.

o The goal for businesses at this stage is to have a larger and more diverse company.

o At this stage CEOs have already figured out/ know the dos and don'ts. Losses aren't fatal, and growth and development can easily be funded.

In stage one, entrepreneurs need to know how to perform well. They are the ultimate indicator of whether a business will fail or succeed based on their business ideas, amount of cash for startup, customer service skills, systems, budgeting, etc. This is contrary to stage five, where there are well developed and skilled people in place to make sure the company succeeds. Having an owner with these qualities is less of a priority.

All stages face similar problems. All stages require change, and all stages will come with challenges. But all stages also have the potential to generate a lot of money.

How to Hire and Manage Employees

If you do not have any employees and have no intentions on hiring anytime soon, you can skip this part for now. Come back to this section later when you need it, or you can read along to get ahead.

Create a plan for paying employees:
1. Make sure you have an EIN.
2. Make sure you have your state or local tax IDs.
3. Decide on having employees or independent contractors.
4. Every new employee needs to complete a W4 form, and this form needs to be turned in to the IRS.
5. Schedule pay periods and pay days. These need to be coordinated with IRS withholdings.
6. Create a compensation plan for vacations, leaves, and holidays.
7. Choose an administering payroll option. Will it be in-house or externally prepared?
8. Who will manage your payroll system? Have a system in place.
9. Know what records to keep on file and for how long.
10. Report payroll taxes quarterly and annually as needed.

Employees vs. Independent Contractors

Know the difference between the two. Knowing the rules and differences between hiring the two will keep you legally compliant, help you know how their taxes should be withheld, and how the hiring process works. You will also be able to avoid running into roadblocks and troubles with Uncle Sam. It will help prevent you from having to pay back penalties and taxes, reimbursed wages, and provide benefits.

The main difference between the two are:

1. Employee
a. Works for your company.
b. Must be provided benefits if working 36 hours a week or more.
c. Clocks in and out at the company.
2. Independent contractor
a. Works under a separate business name from the company.
b. Self-employed individuals.
c. Sends invoices to the company for the work they've completed.

If you hire or contract others to perform work, you must be able to determine if they are an employee or contractor. Visit the IRS website for the common law rules to help determine this. When having employees, by law, the employer must offer certain healthcare and other benefits to qualifying employees. However, some benefits are optional. According to irs.gov,

Required benefits:

1. Social Security taxes- Both the employee and employer pay the same rate.

2. Workers' compensation- This is required through a state workers compensation program, commercial carrier, or self-insured basis.

3. Disability insurance- This benefit is only required in California, New Jersey, Hawaii, Puerto Rico, Rhode Island, and New York. If your business isn't based in these states, this won't be a requirement for you.

4. Leave benefits- Leave benefits stipulated in FMLA are required, but

others are optional.

5. <u>Unemployment insurance-</u> this varies by state. You will have to do more research about your particular state or contact your state workforce agency to determine if you will need to register.

Optional benefits:

Retirement plans are very popular, but optional. Pension plans and an employee sponsored 401K plan are generally offered. Although it is not mandatory, it would be good for small businesses to offer some of the optional benefits to help current employees and attract new ones.

Employee incentives:

Offering employee incentives are a great way to show employees how much you appreciate and care about them. This is optional, so make sure your budget allows for whatever you choose to offer. Not only should the incentives be accounted for, but also the software you would need to invest in to make your accounting process easier. Common incentives offered are Wellness programs, company events, corporate memberships and discounts, stock options, etc.

Federal and state labor laws are in place to protect business and workers' rights. It's important to abide by these laws to keep you, your business, and your workers safe.

Intro to Social Media

In this day and age, I'm convinced that everybody in the world knows about social media. There is YouTube, Facebook, TikTok, Twitter, Instagram and probably more. That's all I know about and use. If it's not helping me grow my business and secure the bag, it's irrelevant.

I didn't have this mindset my entire life. I wasted my time on social media for many years before realizing how beneficial it could be to helping me run up a check. I'd say since Myspace days I've been on social media, but it took me over ten years to figure out how useful it can be for businesses. I hate that I wasted so much time, but I won't dwell on the past and neither should you. It ain't nothing we can do about the time that has come and gone. We can only focus on the present and future.

I'm here to tell you it's time to tighten up and use the hell out of your resources. The days of posting random 'ish on social media is OVER! Falling into the negativity is OVER! And the days of not collecting a bag from it is, you guessed it right, OVEEERR!

Social media allows you to connect and grow with your audience on a personal level, so you can have more influence on their decisions and purchases. Besides, social media is a free advertising network if you use it properly.

It can be extremely beneficial, but being consistent and creating bomb content is key to growing your brand or business on there. Use social media to show off your products and services, invite your audience to events, promote sales, do giveaways, and answer questions about your products and services.

The only way you'll be able to survive Instagram's algorithm is if you understand it. Here's how it works:
1. You post one time.
2. The post is shown to 5-10% of your followers.
3. If they engage with your content such as liking, commenting and/or

sharing, then Instagram starts showing it to more people.

4. Then if those extra people Instagram showed your content to engage, Instagram may put it on the explore page and hashtags page because of the positive post ranking.

5. Then you gain more exposure and grow.

This is why it's important to post multiple times of the day with bomb ass content. If you are posting dope content, people will engage. When you post multiple times of the day with fire content, even more people will engage. This will ultimately result in more exposure, which increases your page followers, and eventually generate more sales.

Choosing Social Media Platforms

Choosing the right social media platform that best suits your business needs is important too. Just because there's YouTube, Facebook, Instagram, LinkedIn, Pinterest, and Twitter available, it doesn't necessarily mean you need to have all six of them. Once you've figured out your target audience, you'll be able to settle on which social medias will work best. Not all social media platforms are created equal. If you're running on a tight budget with less than $3000 a month to spend on marketing, choosing one platform that you know you can keep up with will be the best start for you.

Let's dig into these social media platforms a little deeper. Now, I'm no social media expert, and far from a know-it-all, so what I'm about to share with you are statistics I've collected during my own research.

Facebook has the largest social media audience. The ages that typically uses Facebook are between the ages of twenty-five to fifty-five. Facebook is the best platform to use for ads and are more likely to increase sales.

Instagram is more for growing brands and influencers. It is good for the picture and video content. It's great for building communities and networking as well. Its ads are setup on Facebook and the ages that typically use Instagram are eighteen to thirty-four.

Use your IG profile to increase awareness. This is also a great place to find micro and nano influencers to work with. On Instagram you can support and talk about important causes with your audience. Use it consistently to help your profile grow.

TikTok is flooded with influencers. It's good for short-term content and videos that are mainly used for marketing. The good thing is it has an ultra-personalized algorithm, which means it only shows video content based on audience interests. It's also great for running ads with a low budget.

TikTok has become one of the most popular social media platforms to be a part of today. It's the leading platform for short-video content. Most of the short trends seen on IG reels and YouTube shorts started on TikTok first.

They have over one-billion active users. Nowadays folks are impatient, so TikTok is a great platform to use because the videos are only about a minute long. But word in the street is TikTok is starting to favor longer videos that doesn't use music. This is the business tea I've been hearing lately. Is it true? Well, we'll have to try it and find out.

You can reach a wide variety of audiences and satisfy their short attention spans on TikTok. This is the new YouTube for people who doesn't like waiting for what they want to see. In other words, you should be adding TikTok to your marketing plans and social media content strategy.

Every entrepreneur, even ones with small businesses should have a TikTok dedicated to their business. But remember, anything tied to your business name should be on brand. If you're participating in the bust-it challenge, it should align and relate to your brand. If you're participating in trendy TikTok's on your brands page with no strategic plan behind it, STOP! It's unprofessional, confusing, and tacky! If you want a TikTok for you, make a TikTok for you, but when it comes to that TikTok you set up with that business name, anything on it should reflect that brand.

Pinterest is great for décor, food, art, wedding, fashion, and travel businesses. It is highly visual and great for driving traffic. Although the age group that's on Pinterest is unknown, statistics have shown that there are more women on this platform than men.

YouTube ranges from all ages as young as three years old to sixty-five years of age. It has a large audience and the ads for YouTube are ran through Google.

LinkedIn is good for service-based businesses only. It helps build relationships with higher positioned folks at companies. The ages on this platform are mainly between twenty-five to forty-three. Ads can be run on LinkedIn as well.

No matter which social media you decide on, consistency, creativity, and engagement are important. Make sure you are responding to your audience in a timely manner, uploading and posting at least three times a day, and giving them content to die for.

Creating Content

There are two different types of content creation: professionally created and self-created. Professionally created content involves hiring staff to bring your vision to life such as videographers, photographers, and creative directors. Self-created content is when you, your family, or your friends help capture the content you need. Self-created content, of course, will be more affordable as you don't have to pay high fees for professionals.

Truth be told, professionals aren't always needed to execute dope content. You can create good content on your own. If you have a good Nikon or Canon camera, you can get the job done. Even if you have the latest iPhone or Android, you can use that. In 2024, I'm still using an iPhone 12, and although it ain't the iPhone 15, my content still delivers. If your camera is bomb, high quality and clear, save your coins and use it, period! Grab you some good lighting, a tripod, and a Bluetooth camera remote off of Amazon, and honey you are good to go.

Another way to get self-curated content easily is by reaching out to your customers. Not only will this help build leverage and trust, but it's also FREE CONTENT.

Reach out to your customers and ask for testimonials after products have been purchased. Ask your clients for their feedback at the end of calls. Offering a discount or incentive in exchange for a review is known to make this idea successful. You can create a funnel, which is an automated email sent to customers after a certain timeframe. Ask them directly in their DM's, or on follow-up calls if you are a service-based business. For service-based businesses specifically, you can create graphics for social media with reviews given to you over the phone. There are several ways to get their feedback.

When creating graphics, find inspiration, then add your own spice to it so it resonates with your brand. Find inspiration for graphics from the people who are in higher positions than you, but make sure you're not in competition with them. You can duplicate ideas, but not anything in your industry. Make sure to have a purpose for each post. Having a theme helps to coordinate the entire experience. Make your content relatable, engaging and fun.

Never create content in real time. That's the quickest way to get overwhelmed. Create content in bulk on content days to get ahead. Plan out your days to get as much out of your content shoots as possible. Remember don't put dates or use specific holiday props, so the content can be reused at any time. When creating content, ask yourself, "can I use this anytime of the year?" Think about your brand in totality and not just in the moment.

Try social-media management tools to schedule your content for automating posts in real time. Although there are many options such as tailwind, Loomly, and Hootsuite, I use Planoly. It does cost, but it's worth it. Hiring a social media manager is an option too, if you can afford it, but they will still require you to have a paid subscription with one of these companies to automate your post. When hiring a social media manager, you will also need to provide the content. I personally feel that you could do without one, but you decide.

If you're not creative, then find someone who is. There are creative directors available and graphic designers to help. Your social media profile is your storefront. You want it to be fun, creative, and personable. If you struggle with content ideas, use Pinterest or conversations you have with your audience. Remember, anytime and any day is a good day for content creation. Use your resources and get creative.

How to Create Engaging Reels

Reels are about the viewers, not you. The first one-to-three seconds must be interesting to keep your audience's attention. Use a combination of at least two (Music, text, images, videos, and voiceover) when creating them. Remember to get creative and have fun.

Reels are more visible and more about seeing versus hearing. Make videos that are informative and that include tips and tricks, for better view count and engagement. Watch reels to get more familiar with how they are done and edited. Follow the trends and use trending sounds to get more exposure.

Facebook Reels

Facebook reels can grow your businesses, but they require a little work and creativity. Creating attractive content and engaging your audience will increase your overall ROI (return on investment) for your content. It also increases discoverability and visibility.

FYI, Facebook audiences have disposable income. Give your business the chance to show your audience creativity and how much you enjoy what you do. Always include your business on Facebook.

How to Make Money on Instagram

· Post your products.

· Set up Instagram Shop. Instagram shop is an Instagram storefront to sell directly on the app. Also, Instagram live shopping converts viewers to buyers by explaining products during a live stream.

· Instagram badges. Instagram badges are when your followers can buy hearts on live streams to support their favorite creators and brands.

· Include affiliate links in your bio. This is when creators and brands recommend their favorite products to their audience with links to purchase directly in exchange for commission.

· Use the branded content marketplace to find influencers to work with on advertising your brand.

· Share your website everywhere.

· If you have 10k+ followers on IG, use the swipe up feature.

Tips to Grow on Instagram

Take the time to grow your Instagram. Although it can be tough, it's necessary for business growth and revenue increase. On social media, followers equal trust. The more followers you have, the more customers trust your brand. Use these tips to grow your Instagram.

· When reposting user-generated content, tag them or credit them in the post and in the comments. When you do this, you also create exposure for both you and the owner of the shared content.

· Do not post something, then leave the app immediately after. You want to stick around or peek in every other hour to engage with your audience. The quicker you can respond, the better. As soon as you get that notification, tap in. For most, reality is we are busy and can't respond right away, which is understandable. There are two solutions to this. Either you can:

a. Hire someone to manage your social media to be able to respond quickly.

b. Check in every hour or so and respond.

Posting consistently and quick responses can increase your following by increasing your visibility. The algorithm uses interaction, engagement, and consistency to push your page and content to more feeds.

· Use hashtags. Hashtags are a great way to gain exposure and engage with new audience. Don't use just any hashtags. Use the ones that matter. Even though thirty hashtags are the limit, if you're using ten powerful hashtags, just use ten. If you're using thirty shitty ones, it's pointless.

· Niche your hashtags.

· Participate in the trends. The photo challenges, the reels, etc. Just don't overdo it.

· Do more lives.

IG lives

Lives increase visibility, build community and followers, relationships, and reach new people. While on Live, you can add Co-host, send DMs, add filters, share pictures, and share questions. After Lives have ended, they can be shared to your story, saved to the grid, and saved in your camera roll.

Lives should never go unplanned. They should always be as engaging, helpful, and interesting as possible. Create a plan for your lives to figure out the goal. Is it to increase followers, share your story, discuss commonly asked questions? Have a beginning, middle, and end to your live. Remember to promote it on your feed and other social media's beforehand to increase your audience.

Go live at the time most of your followers are active. Remember that lighting is important, so use ring lights to help with this. Do practice videos with your lighting in the area you will go live in, to make sure everything looks good. Always make sure that your space is clean, and your background should represent the brand.

Writing Captions

Captions are the words included on your post when posting pictures and videos. Start the caption off with a very interesting sentence also known as an attention-grabber. Put the tea in the middle of your caption and the CTA (Call To Action) at the end. Your caption should make your audience feel connected and align with the image. Get deep and show your personality, but keep it simple, short and sweet. Simple is better. For example, a good caption may sound something like this; Have you been wanting to start a business but don't know where to start? Creating a business can be very rewarding when it's done right. Otherwise, you will find yourself drowning in debt, regret, and disappointment. Comment HELP ME down below if you need help with starting your new business.

From that post, I would send DMs on how we can get started and share a link to my landing page to capture the lead (A lead is a person that shows interest in your products or services). When you capture the information or activity of a lead, the systems you have set up, starts working on the backend (more on this in the upcoming chapter). In conclusion, a conversation should be able to develop from your post and caption. Send the caption you're thinking about using, as a text to two people randomly, to test their response before using it.

Your captions and content should be planned out.

Topic: When choosing a topic make a list of industry topics you can discuss all day without running out of conversation.

Purpose: Decide on the reasoning for the content you are posting. Is it to inform, persuade, educate, or entertain?

Deliverance or Pillar: How will the content be delivered? Will it be a reel, picture, video, story post, IGTV, Live video?

CTA: What do you want your audience to do? Is this to get a like on the post, a share on the video, make a purchase, comment, follow your page, DM you, save for later, book, sign up, tag a friend, or use swipe up feature?

Don't forget to include hashtags.

In your captions, **GIVE or EDUCATE 80%, and **SELL 20%** of the time.

Remember, a caption should lead customers into a story, so when they sign up and receive your e-mail automations, it makes sense to them.

Content Ideas

You want to post on social media at least three times a day. Here are some ideas on what types of content you can create.

o Content series or content bucket

o Polls on the story

o Q&A on the story

o Tutorials

o Popular dance challenges

o Branded memes

o Lives

o In-person events

o BTS

o Team highlights

o Live Q&A

o Breaking news

o Astrology/personality-based content

o Inspirational quotes

o Product shots close-ups

o Lifestyle shots put a product in real-life situations.

o Brand videos via IGTV

o Giveaways

o Repurpose high performing content by updating the graphics.

If you decide the purpose of your content will be informative, your first post of the day could be a way of creating anticipation and hype. Your mid-day post, which is the second post could be the most informative, and also send an email with more detailed information about that post. The last post of the day could be telling them to tune in for your live so this tea you've been giving all day can get even hotter. Them tuning into the live is a good way for your audience to ask questions and personally connect with you.

If you decide the purpose of your content will be focused on your current campaign or focused product of the day, then your first post should be highly engaging. Maybe make an opinion about something and ask for their opinion. Your mid-day post should be highlighting your key product or collection that's related to your campaign and educate them on the product. The last post should be a tutorial using your product or conducting your service. This should push them over to buy that product and complete the sale.

If you decide the purpose of your content will be motivational or sharing your story, then the first post should be a motivational post. The second post should show the CEO and/or the team. Sharing an inspirational quote in the caption or your brand story is also a good idea. The last post should be something a conversation can be created from. Such as asking your audience to comment anything they'd like to share, or what's their biggest challenges. It should be conversational and interesting.

Here are more ideas on what types of content you can post based on your content purpose.

Entertain: Share videos, create competitions, quizzes, games and share viral news. These can help with awareness and emotional goals.

Inspire/Motivate: Celebrity endorsements, reviews, ratings, and events. These can help with purchasing and sales goals.

Convince/Persuade: Case studies, demo videos, product features, ratings, events, pricing, calculations, and reports. These can help with purchasing and sales goals.

Educate: E-News, eBooks, Press Release, Articles, Blogs, Guides, and Trends. These can help with awareness goals.

When posting content, make sure everything is aligned well for a beautiful layout, and make sure the aesthetic is aligned with your brand.

I absolutely hate going on social media and a caption either doesn't make sense or words are misspelled. It's important that you do not rush anything you type. To save yourself from humiliation, always double check your spelling and proofread twice before submitting.

Writing meaningful, strategic captions can be intimidating, but once you get the hang of the basics, it's not that bad. Captions are extremely important. Imagine showing up to a gathering and not speaking to anyone. That would give weird vibes, and nobody would want to talk to you the rest of the night. Skipping out on writing captions would give that same weird vibe and nobody would know why you're posting or what to do with your post. Don't skip out on writing captions. They provide direction and build connections.

Write them for every post and keep them short and sweet. Speaking your mind isn't a problem but be careful not to step on toes. You don't want a post backfiring. Whenever reposting, always give credit to the original creators.

When it comes to social media marketing, remember not to be spammy. Doing so is the quickest way to turn followers off, for them to report your page, and for Instagram to give you the boot. If you plan to post just to say/show you posted, that's being spammy. Like I stated before, post meaningful content that serves a purpose. Posting anything is like not posting at all. It's time-wasting and purposeless. You won't get positive results. Remember quality over quantity.

If you are harassing people in the DM's and in the comments to buy and follow you, it's not a good look. Nine times out of ten, they will ignore and block you. Don't do anything you wouldn't want anyone to do to you. Before you get desperate for sales, shares, follows, likes, and comments, ask yourself, if someone was in my DM's back-to-back, and always asking for money, would I stick around?

No matter what, be yourself on social media. When you share your voice, your personality, and your uniqueness with your audience, they will like, follow, and support you. They want authenticity and if that's not what you're givin', they will bypass your page. Don't miss out on the possibility of growth, just because you couldn't keep it real.

Nowadays, followers can see right through you. They can tell if you're faking, if you're trying too hard, and if you're desperate. We all know everyone needs something to talk about on social media. If you're going to be the topic of folks' conversation, you want them to be saying things like, "sis content is everything. I love the gems she drops every day. This chick is down to earth. I love her personality. I can count on so-and-so to keep it real." You don't want them laughing at you instead.

I know how hard it may seem to be authentic when everyone on social media is in competition with each other. Knowing you're not where they are, or pretend to be, can make you feel you're not good enough. I completely understand. That's where *staying down 'til you come up,* comes in at. Don't follow and become someone you're not. You don't know what they did to get where they are.
   What we know is that:
   1. We won't compare our journey to others.
   2. We are gonna keep it real no matter what.
   3. We are going to build our following up, increase our engagements, increase our sales, and become billionaires the right way.

When people see your hustle, determination, your bounce back, your ability to make something out of nothing and watch you build your empire brick by brick, it's respected more. It may take you longer to reach a goal, but that's ok. Everyone's journey is unique. Enjoy yours.

5

Expose the business that pays you

Marketing is the key to generating revenue and having a successful business. Marketing is how you show the world your business exists, and how you snatch new customers. If you do not implement marketing in your business, it will fail, plain and simple. If you aren't going to put the time in to market or spend the money on someone who can do it for you, there's no need to waste your time starting the business. This chapter is by far the longest, but the most informative. You can take your time setting up a legit business and identify your target audience all you want, but your business doesn't matter if no one knows you exist.

In this chapter, we will cover:

- How to distribute your marketing budget
- How to maximize your social media budget
- How to work with influencers
- Understanding ads
- Email marketing
- Creating campaigns
- Identifying sales strategies

- Lead magnets
- Landing pages

Creating campaigns, sending emails, running ads, and working with influencers are all ways to connect with your customers (current and potential) to get their attention. Don't forget to offer promo codes to current customers periodically to show your appreciation. Sending invites to events such as lives and webinars are all ways to get them engaged.

Marketing Budget

When setting a marketing budget, there are three focus areas: content, influencers, and ads.

· Ads should make up 50% of budget. Examples of ads are:

o Facebook ads

o Instagram ads

o Google/YouTube ads

o Blogs

· Content should make up 30% of budget.

o Videos and Photo needs for all content on social media, landing pages, email, and SMS content.

· Influencers should make up 20% of budget.

Before paying for ads, check your conversions on your organic (unpaid) traffic sources such as emails, lives, landing pages, SMS (text messages), posts, swipe ups, and sales funnels first. Always exhaust your free marketing options before spending tons of money on ads, blogs, celebrities, and influencers. When you have used all of your free resources, then move on to paid marketing.

Ads are more expensive, so ads should be your very last option to get the traffic you need. Once you've figured out your traffic needs, you'll know how much paid traffic you need from influencers and ads. (Hint, The *Boss Up Planner* on my website helps with this as well).

Content is used for social media feeds, stories, emails, SMS, and ads. With a tight budget, micro and nano-influencers should be your go-to, as they charge less. Sometimes you could even give a micro or nano influencer free products and services for content. Now, you have influencers to promote your brand, and paid nothing for them.

Hiring a Facebook ads specialist can help you squeeze every penny out of each dollar and create successful ad campaigns for your business. Before hiring one, make sure your budget allows for this. For instance, if you are a small business, with a monthly marketing budget of $500, it may be extremely difficult to find a valuable ad specialist. This isn't someone you need to hire right away. Also, if you cop part two of this book, you may find it unnecessary to hire one at all.

Make sure you plan your content for the entire month. This is called Batching Content. This allows more time for you to run your business, get all the content you need in one day and relieves stress. Imagine creating content in real time. You will probably struggle to keep up. Oh, and don't get sick, because then where will the content come from?

When you plan content for the month, use reference photos. So, on the day of the shoot, you and your team will know which direction your shoot should go in. Use custom and stock images. Stocksy.com and Pinterest are good places to find these. My Boss Up Entrepreneur Planner has a section specifically for content creation. It helps you:

· plan out a month's worth of content.
· schedule your content shoot day, hour-by-hour.
· create your content shopping list.
· finalize your content budget.

This is a good tool to have. The planner makes sure you get the most out of your content day, get all the shots, behind-the-scenes content, and videos you need. If you have not copped your entrepreneur planner, make sure you visit my website to do so. You will need it and for sure benefit from having it.

Influencers are always good to use and include in your marketing budget if your budget allows. When you are starting a new business and are running on a small budget, influencers with 20,000 to 40,000 followers are a good starting point. Sending product and paying them $100 max is a good start. Remember, influencers and their audience need to match your brand and target audience. When using blogs, search whatever blogs your audience likes, then find them on social media.

Sometimes when doing marketing, you will run into marketing-budget redistribution. That's when you must pivot in your marketing plan to make sure you are benefiting from the choices you've made.

Every influencer won't deliver the results you need. If two-out-of-five are, then that means the other three aren't helping the business. You need to find three new influencers to redistribute the budget.

With ads, use the ads that are best performing and get rid of the others. Create more content like the best performing ads to gain success. With content, you should know what to do and what not to do based on your analytics. You should also know what to post and what to stay away from.

Focus more of your budget on what gets more engagement, gained more followers, got more views, got more likes, got more comments, and converted more sales. From the insights and data, you will see what products and services are best-selling on social media. That will help you expand the business and be successful.

How to Maximize Social Media Budget

The average organic reach on social media is five percent. So, let's say you have 5,000 Instagram followers. Only five percent of that 5000 will see your post. Meaning, your organic post shows up on only 250 people newsfeeds. That is insane, right? Then, let's say out of those 250 people, only 80 react to the post. That hurts the algorithm. So, the more genuine, interested followers you have, the more money you can save on marketing and the greater the outcome will be.

On average, businesses spend about $7,000 a month on social media marketing. Needless to say, small businesses ain't got it like that. Due to this matter, we rely more on organic engagement. When money is being spent on marketing, every dollar must be stretched 'cause we don't have much of it to play with.

Be careful not to drain your budget with content creation. Other things to include in your social media budget are your landing page, your sales funnels, etc.

o Keep your production value low and focus on quality content.

o Don't pay for professionals until your audience is larger and you know for sure you will make the money back.

Questions to ask yourself before deciding on your social media budget:
1. How much can I afford to spend on social media a month?
2. What are my goals?
3. What will be measured and how?
4. What type of content will resonate with my audience?
5. What tools will I use?
6. Will I do all the work?
7. Where will social media traffic get directed?

Once you know which social media your target audience favor, it'll be a breeze deciding which platforms to post on. Before committing to a platform, know what it entails.

o Know demographic data for each platform.

o Know what platforms cater to what.

o Ask yourself, does this app allow me to deliver my desired content?

o Do I have what I need to successfully deliver on this platform?

Once you know where your audience is, that's the app that will give you the best ROI (return on investment). Analyze and measure your smart goals. You know that goal setting strategy we talked about earlier in the book? This will help you stay on track with your business goals and prevent repeated mistakes. Don't waste money on repeating what doesn't work. Continue to invest in platforms and strategies that bring positive results and a high ROI.

Look at analytics to measure results, but make sure you are looking at the right metrics. You should not be focused on the impressions and follower metrics necessarily when measuring success. Pay more attention to conversions and engagement rates per impression instead.

Social media is where you will capture your customer attention but know where you want your customers to go from social media. You must have CTAs in place. Remember, social media marketing isn't only with Facebook, TikTok, etc. it's also e-mail and text marketing, YouTube, and Google. Outside of social media, marketing with flyers, billboards, and car decals can be just as successful.

Working With Influencers

Influencer marketing is a brand collaboration with social-media personnel that have a big influence on their social media audience. Influencers market brand products or services for funds or free product. If your goal is to build your email list, Influencers are not the way to go. Using Influencer marketing is good for bringing awareness to your brand/products to increase sales. When choosing to work with influencers, you should have a plan in place before sending products or funds.

When you're on Instagram, I'm sure you've seen your favorite celebs with their P.O. Box address in their bio. Yeah, well, let me tell you what I did. I saw that Sky from Black Ink Crew had her address in her bio. Now, I'd been watching Black Ink on Vh1 since season one, so it's safe to say I am a big fan. I love Sky. She is very outspoken and funny. When I saw her address there, I knew I had to get her my products. Getting her to wear and post a picture in our product would shoot our brand to the next level. That's every entrepreneur's dream.

Let me tell you what I did. I have a luxury brand named Peruci Di Vega.

We sell sweatsuits, face masks, slides, jumpsuits and more for men and women. So, I sent Sky one of our best-selling jumpsuits along with a handwritten note about myself and the brand. After sending it, I tracked the package daily to make sure she received it. Once it said delivered, I stalked her Instagram page to catch when she posted a pic with it. Days went by, weeks went by, and months went by. Still nothing. That's when I realized I'd fucked up.

I had no contract or agreement, so she'd gotten free products. I lost the money I'd paid for the product and on the shipping. The loss wasn't major, and the business didn't suffer, thank God. Although it didn't work out, I don't regret it. That's because I learned from the situation.

After the situation with Sky flunked, I started reaching out to celebs managers by email instead. Of course, these celebs wanted to be paid. At that moment, being in the place that I was in my business; I couldn't afford to gamble on the outcome of paying celebrities $8000 for one IG post. Yeah, that's right, $8000 for one IG post. At least that's what Lil Wayne's baby mama Toya wanted. I knew they wanted money, but I didn't know they wanted *money* money, I was shocked. I still have the email to this day. That was years ago. Being that she has grown her personal brand even more, just imagine how much she's requesting now.

That was a silly ass rookie mistake, I made when I didn't know any better. Don't ever think these celebrities or influencers will feel sorry for you and post your shit without money, cause they ain't. If you ain't got big money and a legit contract, save yourself the L and the heartbreak. I am going to help you avoid those silly mistakes I made, and teach you step by step on how to work with influencers the right way.

First, you need to set goals. Understand the audience you need to reach, and the skill set of the influencer.

Decide on the type of influencer you are going to partner with.

- Nano-Influencer- Costs between $10 to $100 per post. Has less than 1,000 followers. Has leverage in small communities.
- Micro-Influencer- Costs between $100 and $500 per post. Has 1,000 to 100,000 followers. Focus on niche topics.
- Macro-Influencer- Costs $5000 to $10,000 per post. They have 100,000 to 1,000,000 followers. Gained following from the Internet itself like blogging, YouTube, creating music, video creation, etc.
- Mega-Influencer- Costs $10,000 plus per post. They have more than one million followers and are famous vs. influential. They help get brands a lot of reach, and their following base varies.

Get their media kit. This is similar to a resume. This shows how serious they are. The media kit should include their bio and platform overview. The platform overview gives you all the information about their analytics that you would need to determine if they would be a good fit to work with. It should include follower count/subscriber count on all medias, average engagement rate for each platform, monthly average page views, unique visitors per month for website/blogs, audience demographics, and campaign metrics from previous collaborations or campaigns, to determine the levels of success.

Contact influencers. Pick influencers you are familiar with and love. Reach out via e-mail, it's more professional. If they never respond, send a DM letting them know you've emailed them. Once they respond, you need to make sure you can afford them. If you can't afford the influencers you really want, it's either back to the drawing board or go broke. It's that simple. And as an entrepreneur, you should never jeopardize going broke. So, if that influencer's cost is beyond your budget, you need to keep looking. Don't completely forget about them. You chose them for a reason. Sit their info aside and reach back out when you have the budget to hire them. Understand how influencer rates are calculated. First off, it's not called a rate, it's called a distribution fee. The distribution fee is how much it will cost the influencer to feature your brand or business on their social media, based upon their follower count, engagement rate, notoriety, followers' demographics, and how many platforms the content will be published on. Every influencer's price will be different, but it's always possible to negotiate. If they aren't willing to, at least you know, but you'll never know unless you ask. Sometimes talent fees are added as well. This is the hourly rate it takes for the influencer to create content. It increases as the influencer hires or must pay more for the necessities to create the content. This could be videographers, photographers, space rentals, props, editors, etc. It's anything needed to create the best possible content, and that's understandable. We all know time is money. Be sure to ask lots of questions, but if the talent fee isn't stated from the gate, don't mention it. You may be putting yourself in the hole and racking expenses. Instead, you can ask something like, how long does it take for you to make the content I need?

The contract. Get a contract that includes what you will pay, how to contact the influencer off of social media, what platforms the content will be posted on, how long it will stay posted, when the content will begin posting, the takedown date if any, how disagreements or dislike of the content will be handled, who is in charge of the content being posted as well as the captions, how and when the influencer will be paid, who owns the content created, if your business or brand info needs to be included or tagged, what the content being posted actually is, and make sure it complies with all FTE guidelines.

Remember, you are paying for folks to deliver. Make sure they are a good fit before paying. If they choose not to deliver their media kit or analytic information, move on to the next. Ask as many questions as you need to get the information you desire. Don't feel bad about doing it either.

Now influencers also have the choice to work with you or turn down your offer. Here are a few things they look at before choosing to work with brands. Your legitimacy (they will check your social media account for existence and professionalism, your website, etc.), they check to see if your brand is interesting enough to work with, and your offering budget.

Understanding Ads

Find a freelancer on Upwork or Fiverr that specializes in Facebook advertising. There is nothing wrong with working with these professionals, but make sure they are legit and know what they are doing. If you have a bigger budget, hiring an agency is better.

Ads can get intense and complicated quickly. When you're new to it, it can be overwhelming. Just like everything else, practice makes perfect. If you are going to handle your ads independently with little experience, expect to make mistakes and lose money. But if you keep at it, it will be very rewarding.

Know who you're running Facebook ads for.

- *Cold audience* include those who haven't seen or engaged with your content.
- *Warm audience* has engaged with your content and/or visited the site

but purchased nothing. They view products or have watched at least three seconds of a video.
- *Hot audience* include those closest to purchasing. They are site visitors who've recently visited the site and added to the cart, but never checked out. These people have provided contact information.

**The harder the audience is to find, the more an ad will cost to find them.

There are four parts to a successful campaign build.
1. *Traffic campaign*– Gathers website traffic and build audience data.
2. *Add to cart campaign*– Allows Facebook to gather data on the audience who are most likely to visit and add products to cart.
3. *Purchase campaign*– This option turns your audience from lurkers to buyers.
4. *IG follower growth campaign*– The goal is for profile views to gain followers with engaging content. This campaign is done through feeds and stories. (This is a good ad option for a new audience).

Getting the ads right will take time. Month one is the learning phase. In this phase, you will take a loss but will gain information. In this phase, you will collect data to use later. In month two if your pricing is good, you could break even. It isn't until months three and four of running consistent campaign ads that you start seeing a ROAS (Return on Ad Spend).

For social media ads, make sure you have posts that flow together. Use social media to increase your brand's reach, earn data, and collect sales. Make sure you're building relationships with influencers on the daily. And use your insights so you know what's growing the brand and what isn't.

When running ads, use A/B testing. A/B testing is when you test different methods of ads to see what works and what doesn't. For example, running an ad with still images versus running an ad with videos. Here's what you should test when starting a new business or when you're new to running ads:

- Content types: videos, pictures, stories, carousels.
- Influencers: Based upon your post on their page, what's the like count? How many followers have you gained? Are there any unique comments?
- Ads: Check what ads had the lowest CPC (cost per click) and lowest CPA (cost per acquisition).

Those are questions you should be able to answer after running A/B testing with your social media ads.

**When running ads, run Facebook ads only and never boost your post! Do not run ads directly through IG!

Lead Magnets

A lead magnet is the way you capture a prospect (potential buyer) to convert them into a lead (someone who interacts with your marketing). Here are a few tips and tricks for lead magnets.

· The opt-in lead magnet should be an eBook that gives value related to your industry.

· Promote your lead magnet in Facebook groups, paid ads, and ad events for higher opt-in outcome.

· Grow the e-mail list. A larger e-mail list can help keep client

acquisition costs low.
- Ask them questions in the caption before they sign up.
- Upsell without technically selling.

Lead magnets should solve problems for new subscribers and get straight to the point. Lead magnets should only be promoted to ideal prospects. The lead magnet should be displayed first, then add a CTA. By doing this, it will increase opt-in potential because their e-mail address has been captured. With lead magnets, upsell on the thank-you page. FYI, upselling doesn't have to be a product. If your business is service-based, ask them to book a consultation.

A good lead magnet should build trust and give the prospect the desire to do the next thing/complete the CTA. The CTA should be something that is good for them and makes them want to do it. Explain why they do not want to miss the opportunity. Lead magnets are extremely beneficial.

Creating Landing Pages

Most of y'all may not know what landing pages are or may have never heard of them. I've had a business for nine years, and I learned about landing pages six years ago. That means I went three years without using them, and that ain't a hunnit. In fact, that's bad for business. Listen to me, learn from my mistakes, okay?

I'm going to introduce you to landing pages, but I won't get too deep into it. (That'll be covered in part two of this book because it's so intense). A landing page is like a one-page website that focuses on a direct purchase to make it easier to convert the sale.

Here are a few tips on creating landing pages:

· Create an eye-catching design with a strategic layout. The most important information should be placed at the top half of the page.

· Write great content. Keep it short yet informative with enticing headlines.

· Define your goal.

· Decide which parts are more important, then get creative to stand out.

· Decide on the CTA and make it clear.

· Use images. It should represent and set the tone of your brand and excite your visitors.

CTA equals highlighted value and let them know why the CTA will help them. Be direct and upsell before and after the sale.

Landing Page Format

1. At the very top, make sure your Header from your website is included.
2. Top (underneath the header): This is where the message goes. This is the message that matches and resonates with the CTA, which motivated them to click on your ad in the first place.
3. If the purpose of this landing page is to build your email list and capture information, include only one CTA, with a lead capture form. If the purpose of the landing page is to make a sale, include your current focus product with the CTA being an *add to cart* or *buy now* button.
4. Persuade them: Include benefits of having this product or booking the service.
5. Testimonials: Include reviews if you have them.
6. At the very bottom, make sure your footer from your website is included.

E-mail Marketing

E-mail marketing is one of the most effective marketing strategies. It will generate one-third of your income. Get e-mail subscribers with pop-ups, during checkout, and with the lead magnets.

· E-mail campaigns drive revenue

You want to make growing your e-mail subscribers list a priority. Let's say, god forbid all social media platforms go down today or tomorrow, SMS and emails would be the only way for you to communicate with your audience. Imagine how much money you would lose if this were to happen and your e-mail list ain't lit. Not only would you lose the time and money you spent on content creation /marketing, you'll lose the money spent on securing the leads as well. Losing money isn't too bad, you can get that back. The time you spent on all of this is where the issue comes in, because once that's gone, it's gone. Geesh, that's an expensive loss. Think about it.

Offer a freebie of value for sign-up (Do *not* offer; Free shipping, a discount, buy one get one free, or a sneak peek). The freebie should be an eBook that resonates with your brand and something the audience would want. After the freebie, follow up with your welcome e-mail series.

The eBook can be a lookbook, tutorial step-by-step guide, care tips, style guide, etc. These are ways to get organic e-mail subscribers.

Website pop-ups effectively grow e-mail lists, so make sure you have one. Emails that include sales have a 70% higher open rate, and 152% higher CTR (click-through rate) than usual business and emails.

When creating emails, the emails should contain:
· An attention grabber
· Free info
· A call to action
· An upsell
· Product links and images
· Contact information
** The subject line for the emails should always use an open-ended question or answer a question.

For e-mail marketing to be beneficial for your business, you must have funnels set up. Having funnels allows you to make money in your sleep without lifting a finger or making a move. Automations increase e-mail open rates. Once your funnels are set up and done correctly, they should continuously generate income after setting it up once.

Good funnels to have set up are the welcome series, thank you series (when sending a thank you e-mail, it should be personalized and in plain text that looks like it came from the CEO), abandoned cart series, and browse abandonment.

E-mail campaigns should be consistent. Within those emails, nurture your audience. Talk to your audience and get to know them. Make them feel comfortable. This is when they will get to like you.

During the nurturing phase, trust is built. Don't wait until there's a sale to send an e-mail. That's begging and that ain't cute. Begging won't make you any money. Remember to consistently push your customers to the next level without making it seem like you are doing so.

Sales funnels is when the CEO decides the customer journey. Planning what you want your customers to do. It's deciding for your customers before they get to your store. Here's a secret to deciding your customer journey. Keep selling the product until they get it. Start at product A, keep pushing it until they buy, when they do, start pushing product B until they get it, and so on. But always start with something free to capture their e-mail so they can opt-in. When they do, it allows the nurturing process to begin.

An example of a funnel is:

- On the same day of the e-mail sign-up, send a freebie in the welcome e-mail.
- On day three, introduce the team.
- On day eight, highlight best-selling products and services.
- On day twelve, send customer testimonials.
- On day twenty, offer specials to drive sales.
- On day twenty-five, remind them of the special offer.
- On day thirty, they should have converted to a customer by now. If not, continue to nurture them until they do.

I hate to tell you this but, email lists depreciate overtime at almost 25% a year. That's why it's important to build your e-mail list constantly with interested customers and not just anyone. That will help keep your depreciation percentage low. Periodically, remove bounced and invalid emails, unengaged subscribers, and other bad accounts.

Build a relationship and the sales will eventually come. To help with increasing your e-mail sales, use double opt-in methods. Make sure you segment your list, so customers only receive the content they're interested in. Keep subject lines short, clear, and interesting. Personalize messages as much as possible. When sending emails, always include more educational content over promotional content. Remember the eighty-twenty rule? Give to your customers eighty percent of the time and sell to them the other twenty percent.

Giving to your customers would be valuable information, interesting content, and whatever else you decide to send that doesn't include a sale transaction. During the other twenty percent is when you can sell to them. Split the eighty twenty up. Scatter it throughout the month. For example. If you send one email a week, then you are sending four emails a month. Majority of the month would be three educational emails and one sale email. Although that isn't an eighty twenty split but more of a seventy-five twenty-five split, you are educating more than selling and that's what matters.

Website Checklist

Another way to market your products and services is on your website, believe it or not. Even if you have a service-based business, having an online portfolio with a booking app integrated helps. It gives you a way to upsell and collect emails as well. If you have a product-based business, it's even more beneficial.

We've talked about my favorite domain and website hosts earlier in the chapters, so I won't get into it again. I've designed all my websites with several website hosts over the years and it's not as hard as you think. If you visit my website (www.theecourtneysimone.com), you'll see what I was able to accomplish on my own with no graphic designing degrees or classes. I've gotten so many compliments on how the website is clean, straightforward, modern, and easy to navigate. I say all of that to say this, you can design your website and it still serve its purpose. Here are a few tips to keep in mind and double-check when doing so.

- o Is your website mobile-friendly?
- o Are your buttons clickable?
- o Are the fonts readable?
- o Is your background a light neutral color?
- o Is there consistency across the site?
- o Are your pictures and videos clear?
- o Is it easy to navigate?
- o Is your site free from spelling and grammar errors?
- o Do all of your products have images?
- o Do all of your products have product descriptions?
- o Have you created a contact page?
- o Have you created an about page?
- o Do your navigation buttons work properly?
- o Is your website up to speed?
- o Does your website crash?
- o Have you included policies?
- o Have you included a chat option?
- o Have you included your social media hyperlinks?
- o Have you integrated Google Analytics?
- o Are your CTAs clear?

Creative Campaign Creation

A campaign is a variety or series of things that work together to send a narrative to achieve a goal. A customer journey comes before creating campaigns. Here are the phases to your customer journey.

· _Phase one_ is your freebie.

· _Phase two_ is talking and nurturing through emails.

· _Phase three_ is suggesting products for customers to buy. (FYI, this comes after about five emails).

· _Phase four_ is the experience. From the customer service you delivered, to the excitement you've built through your packaging, their experience should be memorable.

· _Phase five_ is advocacy. This is when you get your reviews and feedback on how they feel about your product or service. (It can be good or bad word of mouth shared with their colleagues).

Before you can run a campaign, you need to decide on your focus product. A focus product should be one item per day, week, or month. It's up to you to decide how long you need or want to sell this product/service. Keep in mind marketing will be more expensive if you have more than one focus product for the month, as more content will need to be created.

When choosing a focus product, ask yourself these four questions:

1. What is the best-selling product or service?

2. What products and services do I already have content with? Or what products can I create lots of content with inexpensively?

3. What products do I have in stock? Or what services can I deliver that won't burn me out?

4. What products or services get my audience hyped?

Each product or service should have at least one benefit. Create a T chart after deciding on your focus product to make sure the focus product is a good choice. Decide what are the benefits of this product for your customers. What will change when they get this product? What are others saying about it that you can brag about, and what is the disadvantage for them if they do not buy this product?

When it comes to creating a campaign, there are quite a few steps, but with converting memorable campaigns, it's levels to this 'ish. These are the exact steps, in order, that I take to create my campaigns.

1. Choose a *focus product.*
2. Figure out *monthly goals.*
3. Decide on the *concept* and *story* you want to tell. Ask yourself, what is the key message?
4. *Find inspiration* on Pinterest.
5. Create *mood board.*
6. Identify *monthly goals* (sheet in my Boss Up Planner).
7. Complete *campaign budget* (in my Boss Up Planner).
8. Create *a content strategy & plan* (the plan on what to post on social media and how to post it).
9. Complete *content day planning.*
10. *Execute* with photoshoot.
11. Create *landing page.*
12. Create *Marketing Plan.* Include email funnels for the campaign, revenue goal plan, ads plan, emails, SMS, sales strategy, traffic plan & marketing tactics with customer journey. (Marketing Tactics can include free live training, flyers, preorder, waitlist, exclusive release, buy 1 get 1 free, or 50% off offer).
13. *Create graphics.*
14. *Schedule content.*
15. *Monitor* your results (pinpoint the problem, figure out the solution, and pivot).
16. *Pivot* to make the best out of your campaigns.
17. *Analyze.* Figure out what worked for this campaign to continue doing in the future and figure out what didn't work, and why, to solve those problems.

I know that was a mouthful, but I'm hoping the step-by-step guide will make it easy for you. Take it one day at a time. Cop my *Boss Up Entrepreneur Edition Planner* to reach your highest success. Once you do, this step-by-step guide will make more sense. You can find it on my website at *theecourtneysimone.com*. I love you so very much. I will include a QR code for you at the back of this book. That way you'll be able to find your planner easily, with no hassle at all.

Campaigns can run for however long you want them to. You can run a campaign for seven days, thirty days, sixty days, etc. The timeframe is determined by your financial goals and your budget.

When developing campaigns:
- Moods should be chosen. (What's the energy you want to give)?
- Colors and elements such as fonts, textures, and patterns should be chosen for your visuals.
- Campaign and content should revolve around the focus products or service.
- The content created should be reusable.
- Plan ahead of time to prevent exhaustion.

Sales strategy

Your sales strategy is how you plan on successfully generating the amount of money your business needs to meet your financial goals.

Low-cost upsell-
- Low-price buy, but upsell at checkout.
- Great for new customers.
- Not for current customers with high-paying status.

· Customers spend the same amount of money differently.

· Cons: takes more time to make more money.

Bundle strategy-

· Multiple items being sold together for one price. When bought separately, it typically costs more, so bundles should be considered a deal.

· Pros: sell more products quickly.

· Cons: will cost more upfront for customers. This strategy is good for repeat customers who already understand your value. Not ideal for new customers.

Discount strategy-

· Product is only a lower cost with a custom discount code. Ideal for new customers and cart abandoners.

· Pros: offers a small amount of savings to customers so they can understand your value and see your product.

· Cons; not always the best strategy.

Low-cost high quantity strategy-

· Low-cost product or service with a small upsell at checkout for more orders.

· Ideal for businesses with thousands of loyal customers and have high website traffic. This is also a great option for Black Friday or Cyber Monday.

· Pros: more people will check out because of an irresistible deal which result in more orders.

· Cons: must have the audience to benefit from this strategy. Which means it is not good for small businesses with little to no traffic because a large amount of people is needed to check out to make the same amount of money.

Creating Strategic Sales to Increase Revenue

Sales promote businesses, boost revenue, and make people feel good about a bargain purchase. Sales can spike interest, gain customers, and move products faster. For new customers, sales get the business noticed, promotes the brand, and attract competitors' customers. For existing customers, discounts and exclusive rewards help build loyalty.

Remember:
- Too good to be true sales will run off customers.
- Create sales carefully.
- Use sales sparingly with a goal in mind.
- The sale must be promoted.
- Use bold colors and fonts on sales promotion graphics content.
- Motion graphics promote sales better.
- Use different promo designs and try not to recycle them.
- Create hype ahead of time.
- Make CTA clear.
- Sales example- Seasonal, holidays, flash sales, mystery deals, bogo, sign up specials.
- Go live to announce sales.
- Have a sales policy in place on your website beforehand.

Knowing Sales Timeline:
- When will the sale start and end?
- Are there different phases to the sale?
- When will advertising start?

Ask yourself these two questions before you start a sale.
1. What are the goals?
2. What is more important: new leads, customers, or units sold?

**The number-one secret to generating more sales is exposure.

Converting traffic into sales
- Know the difference between leads and customers.
- Automate emails and set up funnels.
- Retarget with Google and Facebook ads.
- Increase your e-mail list.
- Moving followers to funnels will convert them into customers.

How to get repeat customers
- Know how to turn prospects into leads.
- Convince people to sign up for emails.
- Promote on social media, in emails, and on your website.
- Retarget with Facebook and Google ads.
- Have email automations and funnels set up.

**The goal in business is to gain loyal and repeat customers.
- Loyal customers are worth up to ten times their first purchase amount.

6

Hard work pays off

I applaud you for being a trooper. You made it to the end of the book. This shows you have what it takes to be a boss-ass bitch, and the go-getter in you is showing.

I know this was a lot of information to take in, but you will always have this book to use as a reference guide. I tried my hardest to reciprocate the information in ways you would best understand and stay engaged. I don't want you to only read it but understand it.

Don't forget to cop part two where even more gems are dropped. I touch on more topics such as day-to-day operations, how to scale your business, how to set up Facebook and Google ads step by step, how to market for millions, and so much more. Make sure you grab your copy. Don't fumble the bag. You can also find your Manifestation journal, Boss-Up Planner, and Business-Terminology Bible on my website: TheeCourtneySimone.com

I appreciate your support, and I wish you all the millions and success! Hope to chat with you again soon in part two. Don't be a stranger, connect with me on IG:*@theecourtneysimone* and get to know me and my family personally on YouTube. The channel is *Kick It Wit Courtney*. Make sure you say hey when you get there.

About the Author

"This name may be common, but everything attached to mine is a BIG DEAL"

Courtney was born in North Charleston, SC. She currently resides in North Carolina with her son, daughter, and longtime partner. Being raised by a single mother to three, being raised on welfare in poverty, and then being a teen mom herself, she was determined to make a better way for herself and her family.

She attended college at the age of 17, graduating with an Associate's in Health Science two years later. Although she has been in healthcare for the majority of her career, she's always had a passion for writing. Becoming a published author has always been her dream.

Since she was a little girl, Courtney enjoyed reading and writing. With her devotion to writing, she wrote every chance she got, about any and everything. She also had a passion for storytelling. With the combination of the two, she started writing short stories.

In elementary school, as a young girl, she won a writing competition for the state of SC, and in the third grade, won her first writing trophy. As she got older, due to life experiences, writing became more than a hobby for her; it became therapeutic, and that's when Author Courtney Simone was discovered.

In 2019, Courtney Simone published her first urban fiction novel, "Love, Lies 'N Betrayal" and became the C.E.O of Dream Ink Publications. As she embarks on her journey as a published author, she strives to entertain young adults with material they can relate to, hoping that it will help them cope with the hardships, struggles, and frustration that are dealt to them daily.

Since then, she has also become a YouTube creator. She shares her life on a daily, to connect with her supporters on a more personal level. She enjoys showing how she juggles life as an author, entrepreneur, content creator, and mom.

Today, she is well known internationally for her ratchet romance and hood drama novels. Although she has her hands tied with several endeavors, she has so much more in store for the near future and has no plans on stopping anytime soon.

You can connect with me on:

🌐 https://theecourtneysimone.com

📘 https://facebook.com/officialcourtneysimone

🔗 https://instagram.com/theecourtneysimone

🔗 https://instagram.com/tcs_enterprise

Also by Courtney Simone

Check out more of my boss books...

 **The Entrepreneurial Guide To Success Part 2: For Growing Entrepreneurs**
COMING APRIL 2024

 **Talk Business to Me Terminology Bible**

Get Out Yo' Head Manifestation Journal

Boss Up Planner

Made in the USA
Columbia, SC
22 February 2024